IMAGES
of America

GLACIER
NATIONAL PARK

The Stars and Stripes waves atop Logan Pass in the heart of Glacier National Park. The 6,646-foot pass is the point where Glacier's only major paved highway, the Going-to-the-Sun Road, crosses the Continental Divide. The pass is named for Maj. William R. Logan, Glacier's first superintendent. (Photograph by Bill Yenne.)

IMAGES
of America

GLACIER
NATIONAL PARK

Bill Yenne

ARCADIA
PUBLISHING

Published by Arcadia Publishing
Charleston, South Carolina

Printed in the United States of America

Library of Congress Catalog Card Number: 2005927373

For all general information contact Arcadia Publishing at:
Telephone 843-853-2070
Fax 843-853-0044
E-mail sales@arcadiapublishing.com
For customer service and orders:
Toll-Free 1-888-313-2665

Visit us on the Internet at www.arcadiapublishing.com

Contact the author at Bill_Yenne@msn.com

"Greetings from Glacier. National Park." The large image in the center of this postcard is Iceberg Lake, "G" is Flinsch Peak and Old Man Lake, "L" is Trick Falls near Two Medicine, "A" is Grinnell Glacier and Josephine Lake, "C" depicts bear grass near Iceberg Lake, "I" is a Blackfeet Camp near Two Medicine, "E" is Swiftcurrent Lake, and "R" is bear grass, Glacier's signature plant. (Courtesy author.)

CONTENTS

Acknowledgments

The author would like to thank all of his friends in and around Glacier National Park, past and present, for their help and encouragement with this project. Special thanks to Bill Lundgren of the West Glacier Mercantile, who shared pictures from his personal collection.

About the Author

Bill Yenne grew up at Park Headquarters within Glacier National Park, where his father, William J. Yenne, was supervisor of backcountry trails for nearly two decades. The author spent his summers accompanying his father on continuous inspection tours of the trails, and bedded down on many a summer night in remote locations within the park, from Sperry to Belly River.

He attended West Glacier Elementary School, graduated from Columbia Falls High School, the University of Montana in Missoula, and Stanford University's professional publishing course.

Bill Yenne is the author of more than two dozen books on historical topics, including many on Western history. The *New Yorker* wrote of *Sitting Bull*, his recent biography of the great Lakota leader, that it "excels as a study in leadership."

The Wall Street Journal called his *Indian Wars: The Campaign for the American West* "splendid" and went on to say that it "has the rare quality of being both an excellent reference work and a pleasure to read." The reviewer also said that Mr. Yenne writes with "cinematic vividness."

His 2005 book, *On the Trail of Lewis and Clark, Yesterday and Today*, is critically acclaimed, and led to his being selected by Stephenie Ambrose Tubbs and the Lewis and Clark Becentennial Commission as a featured guest at "Clark on the Yellowstone," the National Lewis and Clark Becentennial Signature Event held at one of the expedition's most important campsites in Montana.

Of interest to the Glacier fans who are also rail fans, Mr. Yenne's works also include *Great Northern Empire Builder* about the great steamliner that still serves the park.

Mr. Yenne and his wife, Carol, a Missoula native, have lived in San Francisco for more than three decades, where they raised two daughters. Mr. Yenne still makes annual visits to Glacier to hike the trails and to enjoy an occasional plate of hotcakes with huckleberry syrup at Eddie's Cafe in Apgar.

A playful mountain goat startles a bevy of tourists in a White motor coach in this classic 1920s Joe Scheuerle cartoon. (Courtesy author.)

This book is dedicated to my father, William J. Yenne (1908–1994), who worked in Glacier National Park through most of the 1930s and who supervised the maintenance and construction of backcountry trails in the park from the early 1950s through 1969. He had dual responsibility for the park's roads for much of this time as well. It was thanks to him that I grew up in Glacier, that I had the opportunity to see so much of the backcountry when I was young and impressionable, and that I experienced it with someone who knew it as well as the back of his hand.

The late Mel Ruder, the Pulitzer Prize–winning founder of the Hungry Horse News in Columbia Falls, Montana, long known as Glacier's pictorial newspaper, was frequently an embedded journalist on my father's backcountry inspection trips. Of my father, Mel said simply that "no man knows trails in this great trail park better than Bill Yenne."

My father was also a renowned storyteller, and his autobiography, Switchback, still remains popular after more than a quarter century in print. Those who remember him, remember him both for trips shared with him in the Glacier backcountry, and for his fascinating, and often amusing, yarns and tall tales. One of my favorites involves his being asked about glacial moraine, the rocks strewn across a valley in the high country.

"Where did these rocks come from?" He was asked.

"The glacier brought them," he replied, truthfully.

"Where is the glacier now?"

"It went back for more rocks."

A group of people on a saddle-horse excursion pauses for a lunch break near 7,570-foot Piegan Pass on the Continental Divide between the St. Mary and Swiftcurrent Valleys. In this photograph, taken by official National Park Service photographer George Alexander Grant on July 18, 1932, we see a ranger (seated at left), several tourists, and saddle-horse guides. (Courtesy National Park Service.)

INTRODUCTION

Far away in northwestern Montana,
hidden from view by clustering mountain peaks,
lies an unmapped corner—the Crown of the Continent.

—George Bird Grinnell

Those words, penned in 1901 by the great naturalist George Bird Grinnell, clearly summarize the magic and mystique of these 1,013,572 acres of mountains, lakes, alpine meadows, and glaciers straddling the Continental Divide that became Glacier National Park in 1910.

John Muir called the area "the best care-killing scenery on the continent," counseling visitors to "Wander here a whole summer, if you can . . . big days will go by uncounted. . . . The time will not be taken from the sum of your life."

Glacier National Park is located on the Continental Divide in northwestern Montana. Contained within it is the point where the Hudson Bay Divide intersects the Continental Divide, meaning that the runoff from streams within Glacier flows into three oceans: the Atlantic, the Pacific and—via Hudson Bay—the Arctic. It is the only such place in North America.

Glacier is adjacent to the Canadian border, and to Waterton Lakes National Park in Alberta. In 1931, members of the Rotary Clubs of Alberta and Montana suggested joining the two parks as a symbol of the peace and friendship between the two countries. In 1932, the respective national governments voted to designate Waterton and Glacier as Waterton-Glacier International Peace Park, an honorary rather than administrative designation. The parks are both now recognized as biosphere reserves, and were named as a World Heritage Site in 1995.

Grinnell's Crown of the Continent may well be the most spectacular of all of America's great national parks. Dr. George Cornelius Ruhle, the park's first naturalist, points out that "Some of the most sparkling wilderness of the Rocky Mountains is held within these 2,000 square miles. It is a land of precipitous peaks, pointed spires, sharp knife-edges and deep valleys whose lowland is wrapped in verdant forests. Several score glaciers glisten in the shadow of mighty cliffs. From the lofty summits, streams glide to the distant Pacific, Hudson Bay, and the Gulf of Mexico."

Ruhle served as chief naturalist in Glacier from 1929 to 1941, during which time he completed the scientific documentation that forms the basis for everything done since. This writer never met George Bird Grinnell, but I was privileged to have met "Doc" Ruhle, who was a friend of my father, several times. I wish I could reach back in time and talk with both of them tonight around a campfire on the shores of Lake McDonald.

As Ruhle points out, Glacier's geology is of particular importance. For the geologist, landscape features are exposed as though part of a textbook diagram. The oldest sedimentary rocks clearly retain attributes dating from the distant epochs when the sediments were deposited, with the overthrusts having distinct fault lines despite their dividing strata with ages spanning nearly a billion years. Fossils present are those of some of the earliest distinguishable forms of life.

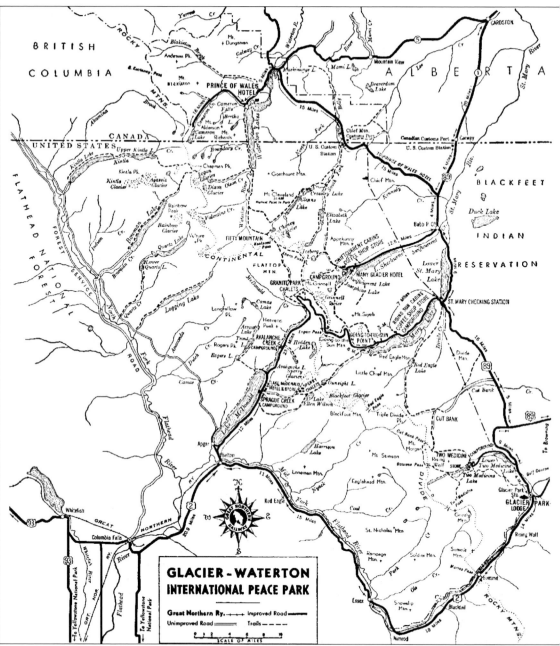

This historic map illustrates the enduring nature of Glacier National Park, adjacent Waterton Lakes National Park, and their institutions. It dates from the middle of the 20th century and indicates how little has changed. The town of Belton was renamed West Glacier in 1949 but is still listed as "Belton" on railroad timetables. The Sperry and Granite Park Chalets, closed for long periods in the late 20th century, are now open again, albeit as more primitive facilities than they once were. The only additional paved road within Glacier is the one that has connected Apgar to the mouth of Camas Creek since 1965. It proved vital in combating the major forest fires of 2001 and 2003. Both the roads seen here paralleling the North Fork of the Flathead River remain unimproved. (Courtesy author.)

10

A young mountain goat looks on curiously as a group of wildlife photographers use high-power telephoto lenses to scan the high ledges of the south face of 8,760-foot Clements Mountain—looking for mountain goats! (Photograph by Bill Yenne.)

Sedimentary rocks formed from deposits during the Proterozoic age, 1,600 to 800 million years ago. About 170 million years ago, the Lewis Overthrust fault began fashioning the mountain ranges that include the Montana Rockies. It was 20,000 years ago, during the Ice Age, that glacial ice sheets covered the northern tier of what is now the United States. In what is now Glacier National Park, these glaciers moved through the sedimentary deposits, carving the deep valleys and sharp cliffs that form the topography of the park as we see it today. The more than four dozen glaciers within its boundaries today are the remnants of this ancient ice sheet. Indeed, Glacier National Park is named, not for the glaciers of today, but for the glaciers that created its rugged landscape 20 millennia ago.

In terms of its biodiversity, Glacier is one of the richest areas of its size on the continent. Glacier contains plant species from distant corners of the continent, the Pacific Coast, the Arctic slopes, the broad midcontinent, and the arid Southwest, as well as those typically found in the northern Rocky Mountains and on the Great Plains. Included are ponderosa pine and Douglas fir forests, dark groves of western red cedar, crowded stands of lodgepole pine and aspen, as well as open parks of alpine larch and white bark pine. The wildlife of Glacier is equally diverse. It is home to essentially every species of megafauna found anywhere in the United States, including the grizzly bear, which is found virtually nowhere else in the country outside western Montana. Indeed, the grizzly has become Glacier's signature predator.

"In its dense forests and on its rugged mountains," Ruhle once mused, "is a rich diversity of forms, types, and associations of living things."

ABOVE: Avalanche Lake, located at an elevation of 3,905 feet, is surrounded by the sheer, 2,000-foot cliffs of an ancient glacial cirque. The waterfalls that spill into the lake include runoff from Sperry Glacier, located high above. Dr. Lyman Sperry named the lake after the avalanche tracks in the clefts of the cliffs. The most prominent peak seen at the head of the lake is the 7,886-foot Little Matterhorn. The lake is just two miles from the Going-to-the-Sun Road in the upper McDonald Valley. (Courtesy National Park Service.)

OPPOSITE ABOVE: The tracks of a lone traveler follow the course of the Going-to-the-Sun Road. The road is buried under snow for much of the year and usually open only between June and September. For example, snow on the road at the Big Drift, seen ahead on the left, may be as deep as 98 feet. In the distance is 8,760-foot Clements Mountain. This striking peak is named for Walter Clements, who worked with George Bird Grinnell to negotiate the acquisition from the Blackfeet of land that became the eastern part of Glacier National Park. (Courtesy National Park Service.)

OPPOSITE BELOW: Gunsight Lake is located deep in the Glacier backcountry on the main trail between the McDonald Valley and the St. Mary Valley. This trail crosses the Continental Divide at 6,946-foot Gunsight Pass, which is near the center of this photograph. The pass was named by George Bird Grinnell in 1891 for its being the likeness to the rear sight of a rifle, with the peak of a distant mountain as the front sight. In this photograph, 7,420-foot Lincoln Peak is in the center, and 9,258-foot Gunsight Mountain is on the right. The Gunsight Chalets, opened at the foot of the lake near this location in 1911, were destroyed by an avalanche in March 1916 and never rebuilt. (Courtesy author.)

13

Why It's GLACIER NATIONAL PARK

GLACIER PARK is established as America's Vacation Paradise—*for reasons*. It surpasses the Old World's most famous Nature-pictures in mountain splendor, scenic thrills, the azure beauty of its 250 skyland lakes.

Here, at the Continental Divide, the Rocky Mountains reach their supreme glory. Go on horseback over wide trails, through sky-reaching passes, join a hiking party or drink the Park's cool breezes in luxurious automobile or launch. Fine modern hotels and Swiss chalet groups. Tepee camps. Vacations $1 to $5 a day.

Glacier National Park is on the main transcontinental line of the Great Northern en route to Spokane and its inland empire of summer resorts—Seattle, Tacoma and the vacation places of Puget Sound—Portland, Astoria, with the new Columbia River Highway and Clatsop Beach resorts—Vancouver and Victoria, and the far-famed in-sight-of-land voyage to Alaska.

Round trip fares to Glacier National Park in effect June 1 to Sept. 30; to the Pacific Northwest, Puget Sound and Alaska May 1 to Sept. 30.

The twin Palaces of the Pacific—S.S. "Great Northern" and S.S. "Northern Pacific"—three times weekly between Portland, Astoria and San Francisco. Folder on request.

Write for folder "Western Trips for Eastern People" and illustrated Glacier National Park literature.

C. E. STONE, Passenger Traffic Manager, ST. PAUL, MINN.
C. W. PITTS, Asst. Gen. Pass. Agt., 210 S. Clark St., CHICAGO
S. LOUNSBERY, Gen. Agt. Pass. Dept., 1184 Broadway, NEW YORK

14

One

PEOPLE DISCOVER GLACIER NATIONAL PARK

The archaeological evidence indicates that people entered what is now Glacier National Park 10,000 years ago. Their descendants are generally part of two distinct ethnic groups who were living on opposite sides of the Continental Divide in the 18th and 19th century, and who live in these areas today.

On the West Side were the Salish and Kootenai people, whose traditional homeland was in the valleys south and west of Glacier National Park, including the Flathead, the Jocko, the Mission and the Bitterroot. They were a Salishan-speaking people, whose language is similar to those spoken as far west as the Pacific Coast. These people were incorrectly identified by 19th-century ethnographers as "Flathead," although they did *not* practice the custom of flattening the heads of their babies as did the related Coast Salish people. Nevertheless, the name stuck. Today Flathead is the name of the Montana county west of Glacier National Park, as well as the river system that flows from the West Side of the park. Flathead Lake, about 40 miles downstream from Glacier National Park is the largest freshwater lake in the western United States.

On the East Side of the Continental Divide lived the Blackfeet people, whose Algonquian language is akin to the dialects spoken in the region of the Great Lakes, far to the east of Glacier National Park. In fact, the Blackfeet are thought to have originated in the area north of the Great Lakes. They are known in their own language as Siksika (pronounced "sheek-sheek-awah"). The term Blackfoot, an improper term for the Blackfeet, has been attached to numerous geographical features in the West, including a river in western Montana and a glacier in Glacier National Park. The Blackfeet people consist of three major branches, the Blood, the Piegan, and the Blackfeet proper.

Historically, the native tribes camped on the lakes and rivers on their respective sides of what is now Glacier National Park. Occasionally they entered the heart of the park, but did not frequently cross the Continental Divide on any of the steep passes within the park. There was an easier route, Marias Pass, south of the park, and another easier route east of Missoula along the Blackfoot River. The Blackfeet rarely went west, but the Salish and Kootenai crossed the Continental Divide annually to hunt the great herds of American Bison, which have been known almost universally within Montana from the 19th century to today, as "buffalo."

The first Europeans into the area east of Glacier National Park were 18th-century French and English trappers, who sought beaver in the rivers downstream from the park. The first thoroughly documented visit to the region by an Anglo-American party was that of Meriwether Lewis in July 1806. He camped within sight of Glacier's peaks but did not actually enter the area that is

OPPOSITE: Shortly after Many Glacier Hotel opened in 1915, the Great Northern Railway invited travelers to visit "America's Vacation Paradise." This advertisement pictures a corner of the hotel with Swiftcurrent Lake and Grinnell Point in the background. Snowcapped Swiftcurrent Mountain is in the center, Mount Wilbur on the right. Blackfeet Chief Three Bears invites the reader to "Meet me at Glacier National Park this summer." (Courtesy author.)

now the park. On the return leg of their epic expedition from the mouth of the Missouri River to the mouth of the Columbia River, Lewis and William Clark had split up for the eastward journey across what is now Montana. Clark went south to explore the Yellowstone River, while Lewis went north. The object of his mission was to scout the upper tributaries of Maria's River (now the Marias River). Lewis named it Maria's River for his cousin Maria Wood. Through the years, the apostrophe was dropped and it became the "Marias," pronounced "Murr-EYE-us."

Because it was calculated to be the major northern tributary of the Missouri, Lewis knew that Maria's River would define the northern extent of the Missouri River drainage, and hence the northern boundary of the Louisiana Purchase. Pres. Thomas Jefferson had hoped that this boundary could be determined to be north of 50 degrees, thus pushing north the border between the United States and the British territory that would become part of Canada. The more territory that could be diverted to the United States by this geographic feature, the more of the potentially lucrative fur trade that could be diverted to Americans.

Chief Mountain is a spectacular monolith located in the northeast corner of Glacier National Park, on its boundary with the Blackfeet Reservation. Isolated from other mountains of the Lewis Overthrust, this lone 9,080-foot peak holds a great deal of mystical significance for the Blackfeet people, who used its summit for ceremonial purposes. Chief Mountain was observed by Peter Fidler in 1792, and was identified as King Mountain on maps published in England shortly thereafter. (Courtesy National Park Service.)

On July 21, 1806, Lewis and three others reached the mouth of Cut Bank Creek. By the following day, they had reached the northernmost bend of this creek, and had made camp within sight of the jagged mountains of today's Glacier National Park, which were about 25 miles away. Lewis waited for the weather to clear to take a sextant reading to confirm their latitude. They were just north of 48 degrees, and named their encampment "Camp Disappointment" in honor of this setback to Jefferson's dreams of a slightly larger America. This was the northernmost point reached by the Lewis and Clark expedition.

Lewis failed to discover 5,213-foot Marias Pass, located immediately south of the present park boundary, nor did either of them enter what is now Glacier National Park. However, three years later a party including Finan McDonald, Michel Bourdeaux, and Baptiste Buche crossed from the west, probably the first time this was done by non-native people. Hudson's Bay Company–trapper Hugh Monroe, who later married into the Blackfeet tribe, is thought to have been living in the park vicinity within a decade of Lewis's camping on Cut Bank Creek.

On August 5, 1934, Pres. Franklin Delano Roosevelt became the first—and to date only—sitting American president to visit Glacier National Park and drive across the park on the Going-to-the-Sun Road. He is seen here conferring with Blackfeet Chief Bird Rattler at Two Medicine. The tribe gave Roosevelt the honorary title "Chief Lone Eagle." Other presidential encounters include Harry Truman's whistle-stop visit to West Glacier during his second term, although he did not enter the park. Before he was assassinated, plans were in motion for a summer 1964 visit by John F. Kennedy. The author's father had been briefed on plans for the Kennedy visit, as one of his routine tasks was that of escorting high-ranking government officials on backcountry inspection tours within the park such as Kennedy is said to have wanted. Mr. Yenne was on duty when Roosevelt visited in 1934. George H. W. Bush visited Glacier in August 1983 as vice president. (Courtesy Franklin D. Roosevelt Library.)

ABOVE: The Great Northern Railway promotional brochure *Vacations for All* was published during the tenure of A. J. Dickinson as passenger traffic manager, and it was one of the most popular vacation brochures ever issued for an American national park. Joseph Scheuerle rendered the mountain in his illustration so as to suggest either Grinnell Point at Many Glacier or Sinopah Mountain at Two Medicine. (Courtesy author.)

OPPOSITE: This Joseph Scheuerle illustration from the *Vacations for All* brochure shows "Roaring Twenties" vintage park visitors engaged in a variety of activities, from hiking to playing golf at the Glacier Park Hotel's nine-hole course. In the center, folks in a touring car cross paths with a pair of black bears near Lower Two Medicine Lake. (Courtesy author.)

In 1853, A. W. Tinkham, part of an expedition under the direction of Washington governor Isaac Stevens, entered the park's present boundaries and crossed the Continental Divide on Pitamakan Pass. The party also reconnoitered Marias Pass. By 1878, when Duncan McDonald carved his name on a tree near the lake that bears his name—Glacier's largest lake—the area was generally known, although not yet widely visited.

Through the 19th century, the exact location of Marias Pass was generally lost or forgotten, becoming more folklore than fact. In 1889, as James Jerome Hill's Great Northern Railway was pushing west from St. Paul, Minnesota, heading for Puget Sound and the Pacific, locating the elusive pass became a high priority. Hill hired John Frank Stevens, a brilliant surveying engineer—and the man later responsible for the Panama Canal—to find this easy, low-altitude route over the Rocky Mountains. On December 11, 1889, less than three months after the formal creation of the railroad, Stevens succeeded.

It was the middle of the winter in the Rockies and the going was difficult, but Stevens kept hiking into the mountains even after his Indian guide left him and, in his words "walked right into the pass." The snow was too deep for him to build a fire and to keep from freezing to death that night he had to tramp back and forth until morning. Two years later, the Great Northern had constructed its lines across the pass.

Meanwhile, even before Stevens rediscovered Marias Pass, some people had begun taking an interest in the idea of creating a national park in the area of Glacier. It was in 1883 that Lt. John Van Orsdale was perhaps the first to mention such a notion. Within a few years, the man who would become the most celebrated champion of Glacier as a national park, was taking up the cause. George Bird Grinnell first heard about the region in 1885 when he was working as editor of *Forest and Stream*. James Willard Schultz, a mountain man living among the Blackfeet, submitted an article about the "Walled-In Lakes" area, the area around what is now Upper St. Mary Lake on the park's East Side. Grinnell was intrigued, and he traveled west to see it for himself. He took the train as far as he could, and a wagon the rest of the way. Schultz took Grinnell into Glacier, where they climbed in the vicinity of the glacier. Grinnell would return nearly every year for the next four decades. During this time, he assigned names to many of the geographical features in the area, names that remain to this day.

This is what people come to see. Jackson Glacier is the only glacier in the park clearly visible from the Going-to-the-Sun Road. Among a complex of six major glaciers on the Continental Divide east of Gunsight Pass, Jackson was part of Blackfoot Glacier when the park was established, but distinctly separate from it by 1939. The rate of shrinkage slowed between 1932 and 1944, but then increased, exhibiting signs of sustained thinning, including newly exposed bedrock. The U.S. Geological Survey estimates that in 1850, the combined Blackfoot and Jackson Glaciers encompassed 1,875.5 acres. When measured in 1979, Jackson was 252 acres, and Blackfoot was 430 acres, excluding glacial patches that had separated from the main glaciers. (Courtesy author.)

In 1955, the Great Northern Railway added "Great Dome" cars built by the Budd Company to its *Empire Builder* streamliner. This advertisements, with its fanciful image of a Western landscape, suggests the section of the route along the Middle Fork of the Flathead River, with Glacier National Park in the background, but there really was no place on the route where the train got quite this close to mountains of this stature. You can see Jackson Glacier from the road, but not from the train. (Courtesy author.)

Another early explorer of the area was Dr. Lyman Sperry of the Oberlin College in Ohio, who began a decade of venturing into the upper McDonald Valley in 1895, and who surveyed and named Sperry Glacier. Among his expeditions was crossing the Continental Divide from Lake McDonald to St. Mary Lake by way of Gunsight Pass.

By the early 20th century, northwestern Montana had changed dramatically. As settlers flooded in, mining and logging operations encroached upon the pristine wilderness of the Crown of the Continent, especially on the West Side of the Continental Divide. In 1891, Congress had authorized establishment of a forest reserve in the area, but George Bird Grinnell and others favored the notion of creating a national park. In this, one of his most energetic allies was James Jerome Hill, the chairman of the Great Northern Railway, and the man who was known as the "Empire Builder." Hill and Grinnell, the industrialist and the environmentalist, made strange bedfellows, but they both saw the value in preserving the area from development. Both understood the importance of setting aside a place purely for the intrinsic beauty, but for Hill, the value was also monetary. Tourists liked to look at intrinsic beauty, and they needed to buy a ticket on the Great Northern in order to get there.

Against opposition from within the state, Montana senator Thomas Carter introduced a bill to create a national park in 1907, and again in 1909. On the second go-round the bill passed, and on May 10, 1910, Pres. William Howard Taft signed off on the legislation that created Glacier National Park under the jurisdiction of the Department of the Interior.

The saddle-horse group that we met on page eight as they enjoyed their lunch near Piegan Pass on July 18, 1932, prepare to pose for the camera. The filming was probably being done for a Great Northern Railway promotional film touting the fun of the Glacier backcountry. This explains why the wranglers are decked out in chaps and spurs, both of which are entirely unnecessary accoutrements for riding in Glacier. (Courtesy National Park Service.)

Unforgettable Vacation Paradise

Cruiser on Two Medicine Lake

GLACIER NATIONAL PARK
High in the rugged Rockies of Montana

What a vacation you'll have in this unspoiled wonderland carved by ancient glaciers. Enjoy rustic luxury, superb meals at Glacier Park's hotels. Thrill to nature's most magnificent mountain grandeur from motor launches on Glacier's sparkling lakes . . . from open-top buses on scenic mountain highways. Hiking, riding, fishing, too. Unforgettable.

Go Great Northern . . . Vacation fun starts when you step aboard Great Northern's Western Star. This great streamliner takes you directly to the entrances of Glacier Park.

For reservations or information on travel to Glacier Park and other Western vacation areas, write **P. G. HOLMES,** *Passenger Traffic Manager*, Department N-18, Great Northern Ry., St. Paul 1, Minn., or consult your nearest ticket or travel agent.

GREAT NORTHERN RAILWAY

Mention the National Geographic—It identifies you

ABOVE: Swiftcurrent Falls is located on the creek of the same name immediately downstream from the lake of the same name. Swiftcurrent Lake forms the centerpiece of the Many Glacier complex, one of Glacier's most important tourist centers. (Courtesy author.)

LEFT: Passengers enjoying a trip on Two Medicine Lake aboard the motor launch greet their friends ashore in this 1958 Great Northern advertisement. (Courtesy author.)

BELOW: A trio of riders from a Joe Scheuerle illustration in an early travel brochure. (Courtesy author.)

The first superintendent at Glacier was Maj. William R. Logan, who had visited the area as early as 1882. He faced the challenge of 1910—one of the worst forest fire years in the history of the area, during which there was no organized means of fighting the fires. He also undertook the challenge of trail maintenance. At that time, the trails from the McDonald Valley across Swiftcurrent Pass into Many Glacier, and the one across Gunsight Pass to St. Mary were the two principal crossings of the Continental Divide within park boundaries. Based at his original headquarters on Lake McDonald, Logan established a small ranger force to patrol the park, and in 1922, Dr. Morton Elrod of the University of Montana set up a Nature Guide Service as the park's first naturalist program. In 1929, Dr. George Ruhle became the first official National Park Service ranger naturalist in Glacier.

Private entrepreneurs established the first visitor accommodations within the park boundaries as early as 1892, the year that the Great Northern Railway completed its line across Marias Pass. Milo Apgar and Charlie Howe homesteaded at the foot of Lake McDonald that year, and Apgar founded the lakeside village a mile inside the park that still bears his name. Soon many others built cabins around the lower part of the lake, and many of these homesteads remained in private hands beyond the end of the 20th century. The great western artist Charles Marion Russell spent many summers at his cabin on the lake before he passed away in 1926.

In 1895, George Snyder constructed a hotel on the west shore of Lake McDonald, about nine miles from Apgar, and initiated boat service on the lake. In 1906, the hotel was acquired by John E. Lewis, who replaced Snyder's facility with a much larger lodge that still exists. As soon as a bridge was constructed across the Middle Fork of the Flathead River in 1897, hotel patrons could take the stage from the Great Northern station at Belton to Apgar, and the boat the rest of the way. This opened the West Side of Glacier National Park to routine visitation for the first time.

George Alexander Grant took this photograph of an early trailer traveler at the Big Drift, near Logan Pass, on the Going-to-the-Sun Road on July 12, 1933. (Courtesy National Park Service.)

LEFT: During a summertime traffic jam atop Logan Pass in the 1950s, private automobiles and a line of Glacier Park Company tour buses stop for a bit of fun in the snow and perhaps an impromptu snowball fight. (Courtesy author.)

BELOW: The John Stevens monument was erected on Marias Pass in 1925. (Courtesy author.)

As described in detail in the chapters that follow, most of the major lodges and chalets in and near Glacier were constructed by the Great Northern Railway Company in the early years after the designation of Glacier as a national park. Eventually, Glacier and the adjacent Waterton Lakes National Park would have more than their share of legendary grand lodges. Yellowstone, Yosemite, and Grand Canyon would each have its singular signature great lodge—the Old Faithful Inn, the Ahwahnee, and El Tovar. Glacier and Waterton have *four*, with three of these in Glacier.

Though the railroad would eventually sell these four properties to the United States government, the Great Northern's Glacier Park Hotel Company would manage the hotels until 1957, when Minneapolis construction company executive Donald Knutson took over the contract. In 1960, management was assumed by the Arizona-based Glacier Park Incorporated, founded by entrepreneur Don Hummel. After two decades under Hummel's leadership, Glacier Park Incorporated was sold to Greyhound Food Management in 1981, which in turn became a division of the Viad Corporation.

Although they presented an ongoing maintenance challenge, the four grand hotels of Glacier and Waterton, as well as three motor lodges, would continue to be just as popular in the 21st century as they had been when they were created in the early 20th century.

The author's daughter, Annalisa Yenne, enjoys a ride on the trail between Many Glacier and Poia Lake on August 18, 1996. (Photograph by Bill Yenne.)

A snowcapped Mount Cannon, with an elevation of 8,952 feet, is reflected in Lake McDonald during a winter long ago. (Courtesy author.)

Two

ON THE WEST SIDE

People familiar with Glacier National Park think of it in terms of two distinctly different parts. To the west is an area characterized by dense cedar forests, and greater rainfall that faces a continuously mountainous, forested country stretching for 200 miles into Washington. To the east is a drier climate, characterized more by groves of aspen than tall conifers, that looks directly onto the windswept Great Plains.

The West Side begins at the town of West Glacier, located on the Middle Fork of the Flathead River, which in turn forms the southern boundary of the park. The former Great Northern (now Burlington Northern Santa Fe) rail line, and the section of U.S. Highway 2 that was completed in 1930 run parallel to the river along this boundary. The town was known as Belton for the first half of the 20th century and was renamed to the more obvious and public-relations-friendly West Glacier on October 1, 1949, coincidently the same day that this author was born. The Great Northern Railway continued to call it Belton, and it is still known as such on current railroad timetables. It is thought to have been founded in about 1890 by Daniel Webster Bell, and may have originally been known as Bell Town.

Even before Glacier achieved national park status, Louis Hill, son of Great Northern founder Jim Hill, and the railroad's president from 1907 to 1919, was in the midst of planning a network of tourist hostelries throughout Glacier to be served by the railroad. His plan for hotels in the park was the most ambitious of any such strategy for an American national park. Until after World War II, the Railroad spent more money on infrastructure within the park than did the National Park Service. The Great Northern would build several hotels and chalets in Glacier, including two major grand hotels on the East Side, but the first hotel would be at Belton. When he visited the area in 1909, Louis Hill had been reminded of Switzerland, and this guided his decision that the architecture of his lodges should be in keeping with a Swiss alpine theme.

The first buildings in Hill's eventual 34-room chalet complex adjacent to the Great Northern depot in Belton, opened in June 1910, a month after Glacier became a park. The Chalets operated until World War II, when all of the Great Northern facilities were closed for four seasons. Sold in 1946, the Belton Chalets thereafter went through a variety of owners. The place operated as Peter Pence's Pizza Parlor during the 1960s, when the author spent many a night hanging out here. In the 1970s and 1980s, they were owned by the Luding family who operated the former Great Northern chalets at Sperry and Granite Park. In 1997, the Belton Chalets were acquired by Andy Baxter and Cas Still, who undertook a massive remodeling effort to restore them to their original glory.

Across the tracks and across U.S. Highway 2 from the Belton Chalets was the original Belton town site. The center of the town shifted about a quarter of a mile to the west in 1938, with the construction of a new bridge across the Middle Fork of the Flathead, and the West Glacier Mercantile, a complex of stores that still form the heart of "downtown" West Glacier. In 1946, the Mercantile was purchased by Dave Thompson and the Lundgren brothers—Ev, Con, and Dan—and it is still owned by the family. Though the years, local young people have secured summer employment at the Mercantile, one of them having been this author.

Immediately across the Middle Fork from West Glacier, one sets foot in Glacier National Park, with the Park Headquarters immediately inside the boundary. In addition to administrative facilities, there is housing for park employees, and it was here that the author lived until graduating from high school and moving off to Missoula.

The town of Apgar lies at the foot of Lake McDonald, just over two miles inside the park. The area to the north and west of Apgar and Lake McDonald contains the eastern drainage of the North Fork of the Flathead River, which forms the western border of Glacier National Park. The region of this watershed on both sides of the river is referred to locally as "The North Fork." An unimproved, mostly gravel road runs parallel to the river within the Flathead National Forest on the opposite side from the park all the way north to the Canadian border. A paved road completed in 1965 and known as the Camas Creek Road links Apgar to the this road.

The portion of the North Fork within the park contains about a quarter of the park's area, and is generally remote and lightly traveled. It is crossed by the single, unpaved Inside North Fork Road, which evolved out of an old wagon road that existed at the turn of the 20th century. Proposals to pave this road came and went throughout the 20th century, but the National Park Service prefers to keep the road in a "primitive" state, and to keep its side of the North Fork remote. It is a strictly seasonal road that is not plowed during the heavy snows of the winter. Within Glacier's North Fork are a series of lakes that are geographically parallel to Lake McDonald—Logging, Quartz, Bowman, and Kintla. Only the latter two are reachable by side roads from the Inside North Fork Road. The latter crosses the streams by way of which these lakes drain into the North Fork of the Flathead. It is about 20 miles from Apgar to Logging Creek, 22 miles to Quartz Creek, 28 miles to Bowman Creek, and 40 miles to Kintla Creek. The Inside North Fork Road ends at Kintla, about four miles over rugged Starvation Ridge, south of the Canadian border.

Among Glacier's grand hotels, the only one located on the West Side, and the only one not built by the Great Northern, is the Lake McDonald Hotel, located on the east shore of Lake McDonald, eight miles north of Apgar, on the site of the old George Snyder hotel, which fur trader and hotel operator John E. Lewis acquired in 1906. The present hotel was designed for Lewis by Kirtland Cutter, expressly to rival the Great Northern hotels in scale and amenities, and built in 1913–1914. The 64-room facility was first known officially as the Glacier Hotel, and informally as the Lewis Hotel.

ABOVE: "Winter on the West Side." A blanket of snow turns this view of McDonald Creek into a tranquil and idyllic scene typical of Glacier in the winter. (Courtesy National Park Service.)

OPPOSITE: The town of Belton is pictured in the 1920s, with the Belton Chalets in the foreground. The hotel and store complex in the center are long gone, but several of the other structures survive. (Courtesy Bill Lundgren, West Glacier Mercantile.)

BELOW: The Belton Chalets were the first Great Northern Railway hostelry to open near Glacier National Park. Like the Glacier Park Lodge, they were on railroad property just outside the park boundary. The Glacier Park Lodge was at the east entrance to the park, while the Belton Chalets anchored the West Side. (Courtesy Bill Lundgren, West Glacier Mercantile.)

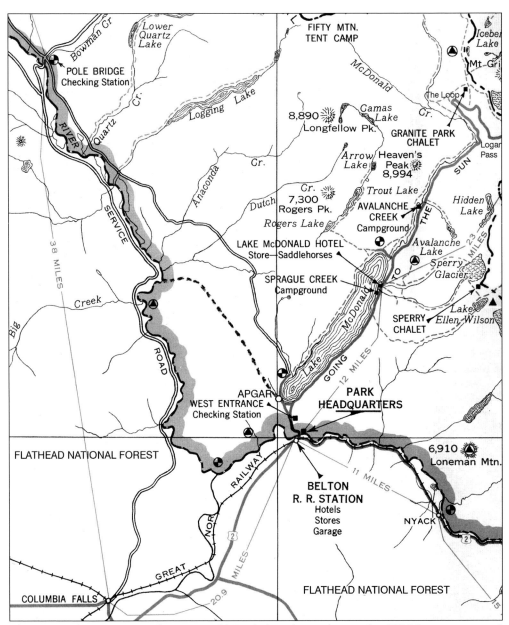

The West Side centers on Lake McDonald. Little has changed since this USGS map was issued in 1940, but Belton became West Glacier in 1949. U.S. Highway 2 still parallels the southern edge of the park and the Middle Fork of the Flathead. The North Fork of the Flathead forms the western boundary of the park, and the two flow together just west of West Glacier. The Going-to-the-Sun Road starts at West Glacier and crosses the park. Built in 1965 and penciled in as a dashed line on this map, the Camas Creek Road now heads northwest from Apgar. See Appendix A for accurate elevations of higher mountains. (Courtesy Yenne family.)

OPPOSITE: The author and a friend are pictured with the author's father (right), near Apgar Fire Lookout, then located atop 6,651-foot Apgar Mountain, high above Lake McDonald in August 1960, with the peaks of the Lewis Range in the distance. (Courtesy Yenne family.)

Over the course of more than a decade, John E. Lewis and Louis Hill coexisted. The latter owned major facilities on the East Side, so there was no direct competition. At various times, Hill considered building his own Lake McDonald hotel, or buying Lewis out, but for years, the status quo remained. It was not until the rival Chicago, Milwaukee & St. Paul Railroad approached John E. Lewis that the Great Northern board of directors were shaken into action. The deal was closed in time for the Great Northern to take over at Lake McDonald at the start of the 1930 season.

Even as work was progressing on his grand hotels and his network of chalets, Louis Hill was planning a series of chalets deep in the backcountry of Glacier National Park at locations that were—and still are—accessible only on foot or on horseback. The seeds for this scheme had been sown in Hill's imagination by Lyman Sperry.

In the course of his work, in which he discovered the glacier that was later named for him, Sperry surveyed the Gunsight Pass Trail and gave Louis Hill suggestions for two backcountry lodges. A chalet at Gunsight Lake, east of the Continental Divide was completed in 1911, and the Sperry Chalets, near Sperry Glacier opened in 1914. The end of the largest structure in the complex has the letters "G.N.Ry." (Great Northern Railway) laid out in light-colored stone that contrasts with the dark red stone of the rest of the structure. Meanwhile, the Great Northern Railway paid for construction of the Gunsight Pass Trail.

In 1915, another high-country facility, Granite Park Chalets, was completed on the Swiftcurrent Pass Trail leading from Lake McDonald to Many Glacier. Both Sperry and Granite Park Chalets presented a challenge. Since they were above the timberline, stone, rather than log, structures were required. Great Northern Railway quarrying crews worked on site to put up the completely native stone structures. Other materials—ranging from cement, to furniture, to food—came up from below on 60-horse pack strings. The Gunsight Chalets were destroyed in a massive avalanche in 1916 and never rebuilt, but both the Sperry and Granite Park Chalets were still in service in the 21st century, and still reachable only by trail.

What is perhaps most amazing about the two major grand lodges and nine smaller chalets that Louis Hill built in Glacier National Park was not simply that they were built in some of the most difficult terrain imaginable, but they were all in service in the space of just five years. It is a testament to the can-do work ethic that was standard operating procedure for the engineers and builders of the Great Northern Railway.

501. Belton, Montana

LEFT: In 1938, Belton got a new main street—as a new bridge across the Middle Fork of the Flathead was built—and a new downtown—as the buildings of the West Glacier Mercantile complex were constructed. In 1949, the town would get a new name—West Glacier. This view from the Great Northern Railway overpass has changed little since this picture was taken in 1938. The bridge was destroyed in the Great Flood of 1964, but it was promptly replaced. The fire lookout atop Apgar Mountain can be seen in the background. (Courtesy author.)

OPPOSITE BELOW: The West Glacier Mercantile complex is pictured in the 1940s. Two decades later, the author would spend the summers of his high school years working at the Mercantile's grocery store, gas station, and ice house. (Courtesy author.)

BELOW: The heart of downtown West Glacier is pictured in 1997. The birch trees are much taller today, but the original mercantile buildings remain, and do a thriving business here at the park's western gateway. In 1929 and 2003, major forest fires burned across Apgar Mountain and the adjacent area, threatening Apgar village and Park Headquarters. (Photograph by Bill Yenne.)

ABOVE: During the 1920s and 1930s, this log cabin on what is now known as Mather Drive in Park Headquarters served as the West Entrance Station, then known as a "checking station," for Glacier National Park. After the completion of a new bridge in 1938, the entrance road was rerouted and this cabin became employee housing. The author and his family lived in this log house for four years in the 1950s, and these pictures were taken in December 1953. At that time, the streets in Park Headquarters were unnamed. (Courtesy Doris Yenne.)

ABOVE RIGHT: The historic concrete-arch Belton Bridge was constructed in about 1920 as the original access for motor vehicles into the west entrance of Glacier National Park. The road from Belton crossed the Middle Fork of the Flathead here and continued past the log structure below. Even after completion of the new bridge about a half mile downstream in 1938, the concrete-arch "Old Bridge" continued to be used routinely by local residents. (Courtesy Bill Lundgren, West Glacier Mercantile.)

OPPOSITE BELOW: During the great flood of June 1964, the author took what may be the last photograph ever taken of the intact concrete-arch Belton Bridge. Moments after this photograph was taken, the raging Middle Fork of the Flathead rose higher and destroyed the upper portion of the bridge, leaving only the arch. Several hours later, the center portion of the 1938 "New Bridge" buckled under pressure from the river slamming into logs that had jammed in the bridge's substructure. With the "New Bridge" rendered unusable, a wooden superstructure was constructed over the archway of the "Old Bridge," and it was once again, albeit briefly, the primary west entrance. The "New Bridge" was soon replaced by a *new* "New Bridge," and the road on the park side of the "Old Bridge" was blocked off and abandoned to vehicular traffic. The historic concrete-arch bridge has served as a pedestrian bridge ever since, except for a few years in the early 21st century, when it was closed for retrofitting. (Photograph by Bill Yenne.)

ABOVE: During the great flood of 1964, the waters of Lake McDonald rose several feet, flooding the beachfront Village Motor Inn in Apgar that was built by local entrepreneur Bill Mackin in 1956. He sold the property to the National Park Service in 1959, and it has been operated by Glacier Park Incorporated ever since. Alive and well today, the Village Inn has not been flooded again in nearly half a century and it is still a favorite with park visitors because all of its 36 rooms offer spectacular views of Lake McDonald. (Photograph by Bill Yenne.)

OPPOSITE ABOVE: Pictured is the West Glacier School's combined first- and second-grade class in 1955, with the author third from left in the top row. The original school building was replaced by a structure that survived a quarter century before being destroyed by fire. The present school was completed in 1988, with a gymnasium added in 1992. During the 1950s, the original school accommodated six grades in three classrooms. Today six grades are taught in two rooms, and there is a separate kindergarten class three days a week. (Courtesy author.)

OPPOSITE BELOW: Downtown Apgar Village as it appeared in 1979. Today it remains little changed from the way it appeared when the author was growing up a mile from here in the mid-20th century. At that time, though, Eddie's Cafe and the adjacent store were still owned and operated by their founder, Eddie Brewster. (Photograph by Bill Yenne.)

ABOVE: Snowcapped peaks are reflected in Lake McDonald on a quiet autumn day. On the left are 8,850-foot Mount Vaught and 8,413-foot Mount McPartland, both named for men who worked in the area in the early days. Glacier's largest lake is named for Duncan McDonald, son of Angus McDonald of the Hudson's Bay Company, who carved his name on a tree near the lake in about 1878. Previously the lake had been named for General Alfred Terry, but when visitors repeatedly saw McDonald's name on the tree, it became McDonald's Lake. (Courtesy author.)

OPPOSITE ABOVE: The Lake McDonald Hotel was built by John Lewis in 1914 as the Glacier Park Hotel. Located on the site of George Snyder's 1895 hotel, it was sold to the Great Northern Railway in 1930. Through the years, there were many changes to the opposite side, especially around the main entrance, but these were restored to their original configuration in a major renovation in the 1990s. Today the lakefront facade appears much as it does in this picture, although the young trees seen here have grown up considerably. The wing on the right is the main dining room, which was heavily damaged in the great flood of 1964. During that flood, the author accompanied his father, who spent the better part of one day dynamiting logjams in order to rechannel the raging waters of Snyder Creek away from the hotel itself. This limited the damage to the dining room, and prevented major harm to the main building. (Courtesy author.)

OPPOSITE BELOW: The interior of the Lake McDonald Hotel during its heyday under the ownership of founder John Lewis. He was an avid hunter, and the lobby included items from his immense collection of stuffed wildlife that he had hunted himself or had traded for. Today the lobby still contains many of these items and similar ones that were acquired to replace ones that have gone missing through the years. (Courtesy author.)

ABOVE: Deep in the North Fork country on the West Side are two of Glacier's highest peaks: 10,110-foot Kintla and 9,810-foot Kinnerly, which have Agassiz Glacier on their eastern slopes. Originally applied to the lake of the same name, the term "kintla" comes from the Kootenai word implying that if you fall in, you can never get out. This interpretation is based on an old story of someone who fell into the lake, and his body never surfaced. (Courtesy National Park Service.)

OPPOSITE ABOVE: The gray wolf (*Canis lupus*), sometimes referred to as the timber wolf, is America's largest canine carnivore. By the late 20th century, it had disappeared from the large western national parks such as Yellowstone and Glacier. In the 1990s, the National Park Service undertook a controversial policy of reintroducing them into the Yellowstone ecosystem. Meanwhile a strange thing happened in Glacier—Wolves began reintroducing themselves! Originating with animals that migrated from British Columbia, at least three packs were living in or spending part of their time within the boundaries of the park, mainly in the North Fork area, at the turn of the century. (Courtesy U.S. Fish and Wildlife Service.)

OPPOSITE BELOW: The elk, or wapiti (*Cervus elaphus*), can be been in open forests and meadows on both sides of the park. They are second only to the moose in size among members of the deer family in North America. As with most deer, elk are primarily nocturnal but are active at dawn and dusk. They prefer open woodlands and typically avoid the dense, unbroken forests preferred by deer. (Courtesy U.S. Fish and Wildlife Service.)

Lake McDonald is seen from Apgar, looking northeast. On the left, running parallel to the lake, are the low hills of Howe Ridge with an elevation of 5,162 feet, about 2,000 feet above lake level. The tall mountain on the left is Mount Vaught, with 7,750-foot Stanton Mountain this side of it and seeming to be part of it from this angle. The tall mountain on the right is 8,952-foot Mount Cannon. Out of sight to the right is 8,565-foot Mount Brown. (Photograph by Bill Yenne.)

A touring car full of tourists heads from Apgar to the Lake McDonald Hotel. The house with the buffalo skull across the lake is Bull Head Lodge, where the artist Charles M. Russell summered most years until his death in 1926. (Courtesy author.)

These wide-angle panoramic images were taken from the Mount Brown Fire Lookout on August 22, 1935. Lake McDonald dominates the top image, looking toward the southwest. Next is the view across the Avalanche Basin, with the Garden Wall in the distance. The bottom view is to the southeast, past Edwards Mountain. These images provide a good idea of the 360-degree view from a fire lookout typical of those which existed throughout Glacier National Park through most of the 20th century. (Courtesy National Park Service via U.S. Geological Survey.)

THE BEARS OF GLACIER NATIONAL PARK

Bears are the most widely discussed wildlife species in Glacier National Park, though they are far less visible today than they were in the 1950s and 1960s, when the National Park Service condoned the dangerous practice of allowing tourists to feed black bears from their cars, as seen in the old photograph below. There two types of bears found in the park today, the American black bear (*Ursus americanus*), and the grizzly bear (*Ursus arctos horribilis*). Both are omnivorous, subsisting primarily on green vegetation, wild fruits and berries, as well as meat. Both species must eat enough to store huge amounts of fat needed to sustain them through their long winter hibernation.

Except for their both being hibernating omnivores, the two types of bears are quite different. Male black bears might weigh from 150 to 400 pounds, while females weigh 125 to 250 pounds. Male grizzlies may weigh 400 to 1,000 pounds, with females ranging between 200 to 600 pounds.

Black bears have small eyes, rounded ears, a long snout, a large body, and a short tail. Their shaggy hair varies in shade, but most black bears are indeed black or a darker shade of brown. They can run as fast as 25 miles per hour while they chase prey, and they are skillful tree climbers. They are generally non-aggressive except when injured, protecting their young, or protecting themselves. They can flourish on naturally available food sources, but will raid campgrounds and parked cars if they detect the presence of food.

Unlike the black bear, the grizzly bears have a rather concave face, high-humped shoulders, and long, curved claws that make it difficult for a grizzly to climb a tree. They also have shorter, rounder ears than the black bear. The grizzly's thick fur, which varies from light brown or cinnamon to nearly black, sometimes appears frosty, hence the name "grizzly," or the less common appellation, "silvertip."

Grizzlies are extremely strong and have good endurance. They can kill a cow with one blow, outrun a horse, outswim any land mammal, including humans, and drag a dead elk uphill. The grizzly may be active at any time of the day, but generally forages in the morning and evening, and rests in dense cover by day.

ABOVE LEFT: This early Joe Scheuerle sketch shows what *not* to do with a bear. Provoking a bear, or getting too close when snapping a photograph, can be extremely dangerous. (Courtesy author.)

BELOW: Glacier, as well as Yellowstone, Yosemite and other parks, tolerated the feeding of black bears from cars until the 1960s. (Courtesy author.)

Grizzlies are both the most celebrated and the most feared of Glacier's large mammals. (Courtesy U.S. Fish and Wildlife Service.)

Today the grizzly bear is found in only about two percent of its original range in the lower 48 United States. Between 1800 and 1975, grizzly bear populations in the lower 48 United States are thought to have decreased from estimates of more than 50,000 to roughly 1,000. The highest concentration is in the northwestern Montana Rockies, in and around Glacier National Park, where studies done in 2000 indicated a population in excess of 400. There are an estimated 250 grizzlies in or around Yellowstone National Park.

Grizzly bears have long been considered the most dangerous land mammal in North America, and this is probably true, although real danger of attack from this animal is often exaggerated. In general, all bears attempt to avoid human contact and will not attack unless startled at close quarters with young or when engrossed in a search for food. However, grizzlies are very unpredictable and impulsive in temperament, and are certainly far more aggressive than black bears.

The danger of grizzly attacks is still underscored by the events of August 13, 1967, when two young women were mauled to death in the early morning hours by two different bears. The two attacks occurred in widely separated areas of Glacier, specifically near Trout Lake, north of Lake McDonald, and at the campground adjacent to Granite Park Chalet. This dreadful coincidence was chronicled in the book *The Night of the Grizzlies* by Jack Olsen, and is still a topic of campfire conversation throughout the park. Fewer than a dozen people were killed by grizzlies in Glacier during the latter half of the 20th century, but there have also been a number of non-fatal maulings that have resulted in serious injury.

Nevertheless, the danger of grizzly attack is minimal, especially if one follows basic rules of backcountry safety, such as inquiring ahead of time about trail conditions, never hiking alone, and making one's presence known so as to not surprise a bear.

This photograph of the high section of the West Side of the Going-to-the-Sun Road was taken just east of Haystack Butte by National Park Service photographer George Alexander Grant in 1932. At that time, the road was still unpaved, but aside from that, this view remains the same today. (Courtesy National Park Service.)

Three

GOING-TO-THE-SUN ROAD

The signature thoroughfare within Glacier National Park is the Going-to-the-Sun Road, originally the Going-to-the-Sun Highway. This mainly two-lane thoroughfare is the only paved road that crosses the park, and is regarded by most people as the most picturesque paved road in the lower 48 states of the United States. It runs for just over 50 miles from the park's West Entrance opposite West Glacier to the park's East Entrance at St. Mary, crossing the Continental Divide at 6,646-foot Logan Pass. The pass is named for Glacier's first superintendent, while the road was named by chief naturalist George Ruhle after the mountain of the same name on the East Side. The mountain was called Going-to-the-Sun by James Willard Schultz, who based the appellation on a Blackfeet legend about the mountain being the abode of the Old Man, Napi, who came down from the sun.

It is strictly a seasonal road, open across Logan Pass only from late May or early June through September. Dates vary from year to year, depending on snowfall, and some sections of the road may be open longer. Only the two miles between West Glacier and Apgar are traditionally plowed throughout the winter.

The idea of a road all the way across the park had been under serious consideration almost since the park was created, and the first surveys were done in 1916. Previously, a wagon road between West Glacier (then Belton) had existed in the 1890s, and it was hard-surfaced by 1912. At this time, access to John E. Lewis's grand hotel at Lake McDonald was only by boat, but Lewis was already working on construction of an eight-mile road from Apgar to his hotel site. In 1921, the United States government took over the project, and the road to the Lewis Hotel was completed the following year. By 1924, it had been extended to Avalanche Creek, 17 miles from the park's West Entrance. By 1927, another four miles to Logan Creek were completed.

Meanwhile, on the East Side, the Great Northern Railway completed its own road from its Glacier Park station at Midvale (later East Glacier), 33 miles north to St. Mary in 1913. This road paralleled the park boundary, but was a short distance outside the park. This road was the precursor to the Blackfeet Highway, parts of which later became Montana Route 49 and a portion of U.S. Highway 89. In 1924, the United States government began work inside the park on a 10-mile road from St. Mary to Sun Point on Upper St. Mary Lake.

Under the management of the U.S. Bureau of Roads, the most difficult section of the entire project, the dozen miles from Logan Creek to Logan Pass were finished by October 1928 at a cost of $869,145 ($8.8 million in today's dollars). When the section of the road from the West Entrance to Logan Pass was formally opened to the public in June 1929, Doc Ruhle suggested the name.

The balance of the Going-to-the-Sun Road, between Logan Pass and St. Mary Lake, was finished in October 1932, but not fully graded until the following summer. The formal dedication occurred on July 15, 1933.

In the early years, an annual average of fewer than 40,000 cars per year used the Going-to-the-Sun Road, but by the end of the 20th century, that number had increased to about 475,000 vehicles, mainly during the peak months of July and August. In 1985, the road was declared a national historic civil engineering landmark, and in 1997 it was designated as a national historic landmark. Since 1982, approximately $18 million has been spent to upgrade the road, mostly at lower sections. About a mile of the high-mountain section between Logan Pass and the Oberlin Bend, was rehabilitated in the summers of 1995 through 1997.

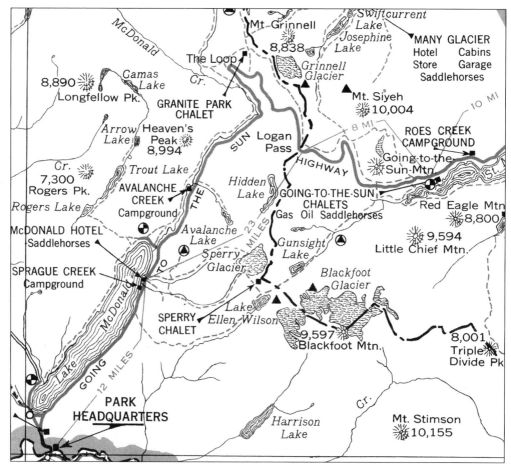

This map shows the heart of the Going-to-the-Sun Highway (now Road) as it crosses the Continental Divide from Lake McDonald to St. Mary Lake by way of Logan Pass. The 11 miles from the sharp West Side switchback known as the Loop (the northernmost point on the road) to the Siyeh Bend on the East Side encompasses some of the most spectacular views in the United States. The Going-to-the-Sun Road also includes some of the most challenging road construction work to have been undertaken anywhere during the early 20th century. Between the Loop and Logan Pass, the road hugs the face of the Garden Wall, the eastern of two parallel sections of the Lewis Range of the Rocky Mountains. This historic map is provided for general orientation, and to show the park as it appeared in the era when organized backcountry facilities were at their peak. Today the backcountry facilities include more and simpler government-managed campgrounds designed for the use of backpackers, which are located throughout this region. The famous backcountry chalets at Granite Park and Sperry are still in operation, although Going-to-the-Sun Chalets were torn down in 1948. Roes Creek Campground, a.k.a. the East Glacier Cabin Camp, has operated since World War II as the Rising Sun Motor Inn. The creek was named for Charles Rose, with the alternate spelling being the result of a misprint on early maps. See Appendix A for accurate elevations of higher mountains. (Detail from a 1940 U.S. Geological Survey map in the Yenne family collection.)

The Garden Wall, as seen from the Going-to-the-Sun Road in the McDonald Valley before the road begins to climb. The wooded mountain in the center is 7,486-foot Haystack Butte. Rising behind it and to the left is 9,553-foot Mount Gould. Haystack Butte was named for its appearance, Mount Gould for G. R. Gould, a friend of George Bird Grinnell. The upper section of the Going-to-the-Sun Road can be seen running across the face of Haystack Butte. (Courtesy author.)

Visitors enjoy a cool splash in McDonald Creek at Red Rock Point, 17 miles east of the West Entrance, and about two miles west of where the picture above was taken. The presence of hematite gives a distinctive reddish coloration to these rocks. (Photograph by Bill Yenne.)

An angler has a rough time
in a Glacier trout stream.
(Courtesy author.)

McDonald Creek is an
archetypical alpine stream.
This photograph looks upstream
toward the Garden Wall
from near Red Rock Point.
(Photograph by Bill Yenne.)

OPPOSITE ABOVE: The moose (*Alces alces*) can best be observed at dawn or dusk, and away from the sound of automobile traffic. Two of the choice places to view moose in Glacier are at McGee Meadows on the Camas Creek Road, and on McDonald Creek adjacent to the Going-to-the-Sun Road, 14 miles from the West Entrance. The author took this photograph there. Beaver have dammed the creek in such a way that a marsh ideal for moose browsing has been created. The moose is the largest member of the deer family and the largest herbivore living in Glacier National Park. In fact, they may weigh more than a bear. Females weigh 700 to 1,000 pounds, while males weigh 900 to 1,400 pounds. The moose appears to be an ungainly creature, but it is agile and fast, as well as being an excellent swimmer. Moose are found near streams or ponds where they feed on aquatic plants, such as water lilies and horsetails. They also browse on alder, cottonwood, willow, birch, aspen, and balsam fir, as well as serviceberry, mountain ash, and huckleberry. (Photograph by Bill Yenne.)

OPPOSITE BELOW: White-tailed deer (*Odocoileus virginianus*) are found in forests and meadows on both sides of the park. Like the black-tailed, or mule, deer (*Odocoileus hemionus*), they feed on a variety of deciduous vegetation, but they will browse on conifers during the winter when other food is scarce. The latter are darker in color, but in other respects, the two species are very similar in size and appearance. The distinguishing features are the mule deer's larger ears (hence the name) and its black tail. Both species make Glacier their home. (Courtesy U.S. Fish and Wildlife Service.)

ABOVE: This photograph of Heaven's Peak was taken from northwest of the Loop. In the foreground, are stalks of bear grass that is the signature flower of Glacier National Park. (Courtesy National Park Service.)

OPPOSITE ABOVE: A striking view of Heaven's Peak under a blanket of snow, as seen looking southwesterly from the Loop. The peak was named by Lt. George Ahern of the 25th Infantry Regiment, who explored the area and prepared early maps of this section of the park in 1888–1890. (Courtesy author.)

OPPOSITE BELOW: A Red Bus pauses at the West Side tunnel just below the Loop during the first season after the 1936 Heaven's Peak Forest Fire, which devastated 7,500 acres of the Upper McDonald Valley. Later major fires in this same area would occur in 1967 and 2003. There are two tunnels on the Going-to-the-Sun Road. This one is 24 highway miles into the park from the West Entrance. The one pictured on page 67 is 17 highway miles into the park from the East Entrance. (Courtesy author.)

The narrow Going-to-the-Sun Road winds its way across the Garden Wall toward Logan Pass. The narrow West Side sections mean that vehicles longer than 21 feet or wider than eight feet are now prohibited on the road between Avalanche Campground and the Sun Point parking area. This photograph was taken just east of the Loop. Haystack Butte can be seen ahead. (Photograph by Bill Yenne.)

A lone rider traverses the Highline Trail, which parallels the Going-to-the-Sun Road several hundred feet higher on the Garden Wall. (Courtesy author.)

Looking toward the summit of the Going-to-the-Sun Road from near the Loop, the road can be seen running across the Garden Wall on the left. Mount Oberlin is in the center, with Logan Pass just out of sight on the left between its shoulder and the end of the Garden Wall. Bird Woman Falls can be seen this side of Mount Oberlin. It is 960 feet tall, with its largest single drop being 560 feet. Bird Woman Falls is named for Sacagawea, the Shoshone teenager who aided Lewis and Clark in a large part of their expedition to the Pacific and back in 1805–1806. Her name means "Bird Woman" in the language of the Hidatsa, the people with whom she was living when Lewis and Clark met her on the Knife River in what is now North Dakota in 1805. The expedition passed through Montana, but did not visit Glacier, so Sacagawea never saw these falls. The upper reaches of McDonald Creek can be seen snaking through the valley below. (Photograph by Bill Yenne.)

Joe Scheuerle sketched this cartoon mountain goat in alpine mountaineering garb. (Courtesy author.)

LEFT: A low-hanging cloud seems to be issuing forth from the crest of rugged, 8,180-foot Mount Oberlin. Seen here from the Going-to-the-Sun Road above Haystack Butte, the mountain was named by Dr. Lyman Sperry for the college with which he was affiliated. (Photograph by Bill Yenne.)

BELOW: Probably protecting her nearby nest, this plucky blue grouse (*Dendragapus obscurus*) has approached a motorcyclist to draw his attention away from thoughts of interfering with her young. The same blue grouse was a fixture at this turnout along the Going-to-the-Sun Road through most of the 2002 season. (Photograph by Bill Yenne.)

ABOVE: The Going-to-the-Sun Road is clearly visible in this view looking west toward the Garden Wall from near Logan Pass. Haystack Butte is on the left, with the snowfields beneath Mount Gould above it. (Courtesy author.)

OPPOSITE ABOVE: Even in late June, it is not uncommon to encounter large quantities of snow on the Going-to-the-Sun Road west of Logan Pass. In the center, we can see part of Reynolds Mountain. (Photograph by Bill Yenne.)

OPPOSITE BELOW LEFT: A favorite of kids reaching though the open windows of westbound passing cars for generations, the famous Weeping Wall on the eastern slope of Haystack Butte spills water onto the Going-to-the-Sun Road continuously throughout nearly the entire summer. Water from melting snow runs through a myriad of small cracks in a 30-foot cliff over a distance of 300 feet. (Photograph by Bill Yenne.)

OPPOSITE BELOW RIGHT: A wrangler leading a party on the Highline Trail struggles to keep a horse under control as the rider gazes at the scenery surrounding her. (Courtesy author.)

This wide-angle view of the Garden Wall from below Logan Pass includes the distant peaks of the Lewis Range. To the left is the shoulder of Mount Oberlin, and below us is the glacial cirque from which Logan Creek flows. Haystack Butte is in the center, but Mount Gould behind it is hidden by clouds. The distinctive peak on the right is the aptly-named, 9,127-foot Bishop's Cap. (Photograph by Bill Yenne.)

This view across the Logan Pass parking lot looks east from the visitor center. Both the Canadian and United States flags are flown to celebrate the fact that Glacier is part of the honorary Waterton-Glacier International Peace Park. A sizable proportion of the vehicles in this parking lot have Canadian license plates. Glacier receives more visitors from Alberta and British Columbia than from all but a handful of American states. Going-to-Sun Mountain is in the center, with the shoulder of Piegan Mountain on the left, and Mahtotopa Peak is in the distance on the right. (Photograph by Bill Yenne.)

Here is the Logan Pass parking lot in 1933, soon after it opened. (Courtesy author.)

Dominating the view to the southwest from Logan Pass is 8,760-foot Clements Mountain. In the foreground is the trail to Hidden Lake, which starts here at the Logan Pass Visitor Center. The three-mile trail through spectacular alpine scenery culminates in a sensational view of Hidden Lake. (Photograph by Bill Yenne.)

ABOVE: The mountain goat (*Oreamnos americanus*) is like a mascot for Glacier. Indeed, the Great Northern Railway and the Glacier Park Company chose the animal as their logo. Look for them on all of the high-country trails, including the vicinity of Hidden Lake Trail, where the author took these photographs. (Photograph by Bill Yenne.)

OPPOSITE: A pair of mountain goats browse near Hidden Lake, with 8,684-foot Bearhat Mountain forming the backdrop. The agile mountain goat can effortlessly scale the sheer faces of Glacier's highest cliffs, eating the lichen and tiny clumps of grass that grow between the rocks. They are often seen at a distance from the Going-to-the-Sun Road and occasionally venture close to the road, especially in the vicinity of Logan Pass. (Photograph by Bill Yenne.)

BELOW: This whimsical Joe Scheuerle illustration shows mountain goats at play near Sperry Glacier. (Courtesy author.)

As the Going-to-the-Sun Road descends toward the East Side from Logan Pass, it passes through the Big Drift, formed each winter by high winds on the eastern slopes of the Continental Divide. The most difficult section of the road to open each spring, the Big Drift typically averages between 60 and 80 vertical feet of snow depth, and the U.S. Geological Survey reports that 98 feet have been measured. The road may be open as early as Memorial Day, but in 1991 and 1995, the Big Drift was not open to traffic until June 23. This photograph was taken on June 22, 1999. (Photograph by Bill Yenne.)

These two views, one panchromatic and one infrared, look east into the St. Mary Valley from near Logan Pass. St. Mary Lake is visible in the infrared image. (Courtesy National Park Service via U.S. Geological Survey.)

The Going-to-the-Sun Road is seen from the vicinity of the Big Drift in the 1930s, with snowcapped, 9,642-foot Going-to-Sun Mountain in the center. One of the two tunnels on the Going-to-the-Sun Road is visible in the distance on the left. (Courtesy author.)

THE RED BUSES

In 1932, the completion of the Going-to-the-Sun Road through the center of Glacier National Park and across Logan Pass opened the heart of the park to many more visitors than could have been imagined just a few years earlier. Tourists could now easily drive over sections of the park in a few hours that previously had taken days of horseback riding to see. The Great Northern–owned Glacier Park Company introduced a fleet of bright-red buses built by the White Motor Company. Operated by the Glacier Park Transportation Company, they were used to take park visitors, especially those who had arrived by train, on one of the most spectacular drives in North America. Motor coaches manufactured by the White Motor Company of Cleveland, Ohio, entered service within the park in 1915, and White was a silent partner in the Glacier Park Transportation Company.

Later, White developed its famous Model 706 bus specifically for use in America's national parks. White was the winner among four companies to submit prototypes for evaluation in Yosemite National Park in 1935. The Model 706 had a more powerful six-cylinder engine and a longer wheelbase than the competition, so it was an obvious choice. They began operations in Glacier in 1936.

Through the years, the buses have been known variously as "Red Buses" for their color, "White Buses" for their manufacturer, or "Jammer Buses" because of the way that their drivers "jammed" the gears of their manual transmissions as their climbed Glacier's steep roads. The Model 706 is 25 feet long and carries 17 passengers under a fold-out canvas roof. On sunny days, there were few better ways to see the sights on the Going-to-the-Sun Road.

Through 1940, 35 Model 706 buses were delivered to Glacier National Park, and 98 were delivered to Yellowstone National Park. The latter were painted yellow and black, while Glacier's were red

ABOVE: Red Buses parked at Logan Pass are visited by a mountain goat, the animal that the Glacier Park Transportation Company adopted for the logo that is still in use on the buses. (Photograph by Bill Yenne.)

OPPOSITE: A Red Bus crosses the Swiftcurrent Creek Bridge, with Many Glacier Hotel and Allen Mountain visible in the background. (Photograph by Bill Yenne.)

and black. Many others saw service in other national parks across the United States, including Grand Canyon and Yosemite. Yellowstone gradually disposed of its fleet in the 1960s, but, except for during World War II when Glacier National Park was closed, the Red Buses remained in service. In the 1950s, ownership passed from the Glacier Park Transportation Company to Glacier Park Incorporated. In 1989, the fleet was updated with automatic transmissions and power steering, but an ongoing problem of metal fatigue forced the fleet to taken out of service in 1999.

The sidelined fleet was donated by Glacier Park Incorporated to the nonprofit National Park Foundation in 2001, and the Ford Motor Company undertook a major rehabilitation program. Setting aside one bus to be kept in original condition for historical purposes, Ford retrofitted the 32 remaining buses with new running gear, new chassis, new wiring and eight-cylinder "clean air" engines capable of operating on either propane or gasoline. These buses were leased back to Glacier Park Incorporated and they were back on the Going-to-the-Sun Road in the summer of 2002.

Four

EAST GLACIER

Among the areas on the East Side of Glacier National Park to be developed for visitor use, the first was at East Glacier, the town that grew up around the Great Northern Railway station that was originally known as Midvale. It was here that Great Northern president Louis Hill built the Glacier Park Hotel, the first of the huge grand hotels that he planned for the railroad's network of hostelries in or near the park. The site was chosen because the East Glacier station was the first place that passengers from Chicago and the Twin Cities could disembark and be close to the park. The Lodge is two miles from the park, and it offers spectacular views of the mountains within the park.

Development began in April 1912, as cabin camps were installed at East Glacier, and construction of the Glacier Park Hotel got underway. Designed by architect Samuel Bartlett, the hotel cost over $500,000 and took less than two years to construct. Fifty railroad carloads of Douglas-fir logs were brought in from Oregon and Washington for the hotel. The largest, which formed pillars (six feet in diameter and 52 feet long) for the grand, six-story lobby, weighed 50 tons. The main section opened in June 1913, with an annex added the following winter. The lobby alone measured 200 feet by 100 feet, and there was also a dining room and 155 guest rooms, including those in the main building and the annex.

In September 1913, the great "empire builder" himself, James Jerome Hill, celebrated his 75th birthday at the Glacier Park Hotel. In 1927, the Great Northern built what is today the oldest grass-greens golf course in Montana.

Initially, the decor of the lobby and dining room at the Glacier Park Lodge featured Japanese lanterns and an Asian motif to dovetail with the marketing theme of the Great Northern's *Oriental Limited*, but by the time that the *Empire Builder* became the Great Northern's signature streamliner, the theme of the hotel had evolved to reflect what visitors most expected, American Indians. The hotel was located adjacent to where the park boundary adjoined the Blackfeet Reservation. Tribal members were invited to meet hotel guests who were curious about native culture. Initially, the Blackfeet were as amused by the tourists as the tourists were fascinated by the Blackfeet.

Known as the Glacier Park Lodge since the 1950s, the facility still operates seasonally, featuring such accoutrements as a heated swimming pool, and the original nine-hole golf course. It is a short drive from U.S. Highway 2, and it is within walking distance of the former Great Northern Glacier Park station, now served by Amtrak.

OPPOSITE: In the early years of the 20th century, the lobbies of both the Glacier Park Hotel (now Glacier Park Lodge) and the Many Glacier Hotel (seen here) were decorated with the Japanese lantern motif in an effort to tie the hotel thematically to the *Oriental Limited*, then the Great Northern's signature trancontinental luxury train. Today the lobbies have been redecorated and feature a Swiss chalet look at Many Glacier Hotel and a Western theme for the Glacier Park Lodge. (Courtesy author.)

This 1920s brochure illustration touted the recreational activities available at the Glacier Park Hotel. (Courtesy author.)

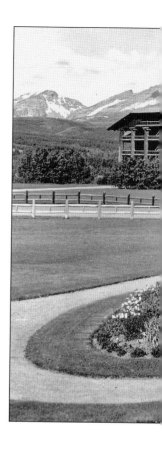

RIGHT: The original gateway structure at the Glacier Park Lodge was torn down and replaced by more formal gardens as the Great Northern refreshed the property through the years. The tallest peak on the left in the distance is 7,353-foot Dancing Lady Mountain (formerly Squaw Mountain). To the right are the more distant 8,406-foot Bearhead Mountain and 8,581-foot Mount Ellsworth. In 1999, the Montana Legislature mandated that place names using the word "squaw" should be changed. The Algonquian language term is an unbiased generic reference to women, but through the years it had taken on a derogatory connotation. (Courtesy author.)

Opened in 1913, the Glacier Park Hotel was the first of Louis Hill's great grand hotels for Glacier National Park. It is actually located on Great Northern right of way, just outside the park. The Glacier Park Station is to the right out of view. Passengers alighting here would stroll through the Asian-style gate at the right and then up the walkway to the main entrance of the hotel. (Courtesy author.)

A group of Blackfeet leaders in traditional attire gather on the broad lawn of the Glacier Park Lodge, for what was described as a peace conference, in the 1940s. The Great Northern Railway's Glacier Park Station is visible in the background. Both the hotel and the station are within the boundaries of the Blackfeet Reservation. (Courtesy author.)

The Great Northern's Glacier Park Station was located at East Glacier (originally Midvale), a five minute stroll from the front entrance to the Glacier Park Hotel. Official National Park Service photographer George Alexander Grant took this picture of the Great Northern's *Empire Builder* pulling into Glacier Park Station on June 12, 1934. For travelers arriving from the East, this platform was their introduction to the majestic vistas of Glacier National Park, and of the intriguing culture represented by the Blackfeet people who were often on hand here to greet the arriving *Empire Builder.* Today the station appears essentially as it did in 1934, and it is still the stop for Amtrak's edition of the great *Empire Builder.* (Courtesy National Park Service.)

This Joe Scheuerle illustration from within the Great Northern Railway's *Vacations for All* brochure focuses on the veritable beehive of activity at Glacier Park Station and the Glacier Park Hotel. In the lower right, we see passengers spilling out of the westbound *Empire Builder* being greeted by cowboys and Blackfeet, as the eastbound train pulls into the station. The Japanese-style gate

Labels within image: Bison Mtn., TWO, OWLING GREEN, PUTTING GREEN, ION

is still in place, with the hotel just beyond. Vacationers stroll, bowl, golf, and play tennis. Farther afield are hikers and folks heading out on a saddle-horse excursion. Another party is driving north toward St. Mary in a touring car. Glacier did, indeed, offer vacations for all. (Courtesy author.)

The Great Northern Railway's eastbound *Empire Builder* streamliner crosses the Continental Divide at Marias Pass, a few miles west of Glacier Park Station. Across Bear Creek, riders pause to water their horses and watch. Little Dog Mountain (8,610 feet) and Summit Mountain (8,770 feet) in Glacier National Park form a majestic background. By the time this photograph was taken in 1960, the Great Northern had been operating streamlined equipment and diesel motive power on the line for more than a decade. The Great Northern began equipping the *Empire Builder* with the famous "Great Dome" lounge cars in 1955. Built for the railroad by the Budd Company, they contained couch-type seating for 57, plus a 21-seat lounge. There was no better place to sit for the 60-mile run around the southern periphery of Glacier National Park between East Glacier and Belton. The author recalls watching the Great Dome cars from the playground of the West Glacier School—directly across the tracks from Belton Station—during the mid-1950s, when they were still a new and celebrated innovation. After Amtrak took over the *Empire Builder* in 1971, Glacier National Park continued to be the key vacation destination on line. Amtrak marketed the park just as the Great Northern had. As had been the case a half century before, Glacier National Park is still featured more prominently than any other location in the marketing of the *Empire Builder*. (Courtesy author.)

This early brochure cartoon shows a duffer flubbing a shot at the nine-hole Glacier Park Golf Course. (Courtesy author.)

The steep face of 8,271-foot Sinopah Mountain dominates the scene at Two Medicine Lake in this photograph dating from the 1920s.

Five

TWO MEDICINE AND CUT BANK

On the East Side of Glacier National Park between East Glacier and St. Mary, the two major streams flowing out of the mountain valleys within the park are the Two Medicine River and Cut Bank Creek. According to early mountain man James Willard Schultz, the colorful name of the former is derived from the practice of shamans, or medicine men, from two separate branches of the Blackfeet erecting their ceremonial tipis next to one another at the lake. Originally, it was known as "Where-Two-Medicine-Lodges-Were-Built," but the name was shortened.

Each of these valleys contains spectacular scenery, and each was developed by the Great Northern Railway for visitor use early in the 20th century. Running parallel to the park boundary on the outside, the railroad company constructed the Blackfeet Highway (now 13 miles of Montana Route 49 plus a 20-mile section of U.S. Highway 89), with side roads running into the two valleys within the park. Inside the park boundary is a network of backcountry trails. Once used by the Bar-X-6, the saddle-horse concessioner who operated a thousand head of horses in the park before World War II, these trails are still very popular with hikers.

As with East Glacier, the Great Northern developed these areas first with a tent camp, using tents modeled after Blackfeet tipis, and then built more permanent log structures designed by Samuel Bartlett. The structures at both sites were essentially the same and were substantially smaller and deliberately more rustic than Glacier Park Lodge. At both locations, there was a main building surrounded by several smaller structures. The Cut Bank Chalets first opened in 1913, and the Two Medicine Chalets followed a year later.

With the onset of the Depression in the early 1930s, park visitorship dropped off. The Two Medicine facility remained in use, but the Cut Bank Chalets were open only sporadically. They were finally closed in 1938, and completely removed by 1949.

The Two Medicine Chalets were a hub of early commercial saddle horse tour operations, especially in the 1920s, and patrons could also enjoy a trip on Two Medicine Lake aboard the motor launch operated by the hotel company.

One of the most famous visitors at the Two Medicine Chalets was Pres. Franklin Delano Roosevelt, who made a national radio address from here during his August 1934 visit to Glacier National Park.

Closed during World War II, the Two Medicine Chalets were lightly used after 1946, and gradually fell into disrepair. Except for the dining hall, all of the Two Medicine structures had been torn down by 1956. The dining hall became a camp store for the use of people straying at the adjacent campground, and it is now designated as a national historic landmark. Today a paved road runs into the park to the foot of Two Medicine Lake, but at Cut Bank, a gravel road extends from U.S. Highway 89 only a short distance into the park. There are seasonal campgrounds at both locations.

ABOVE: Bathed in morning light, Sinopah Mountain is reflected in the calm waters of Two Medicine Lake. In the foreground is the Two Medicine boat dock and the motor launch *Sinopah*. Measuring 45 feet from stem to stern, the vessel accommodates 49 passengers. She and her sister ship, *Little Chief*, were built for the Great Northern Railway for use in Glacier National Park by J. W. "Cap" Swanson in the Flathead Valley during the 1920s. In service on Two Medicine Lake since her launch in 1927, the *Sinopah* was acquired in 1937 by Arthur J. Burch. Owned by the Burch family, the Glacier Park Boat Company continues to operate the *Sinopah* today. The peak in the distance is 8,502-foot Lone Walker Mountain, two miles west of Sinopah. Between them is the northern shoulder of 9,272-foot Mount Rockwell. (Courtesy National Park Service.)

OPPOSITE ABOVE: A park visitor enjoys a pleasant summer afternoon at the Two Medicine Chalet during the 1930s. Sinopah Mountain can be seen beyond the lake. In the Blackfeet language, Sinopah means "kit fox." (Courtesy author.)

OPPOSITE BELOW: In this 1920s photograph, Blackfeet people erect a medicine lodge at the foot of Two Medicine Lake. The location was an important Blackfeet ceremonial site well before the creation of Glacier National Park. In the background is the southern face of 9,513-foot Rising Wolf Mountain, named for Sinopah's husband. Sinopah was the daughter of the important Blackfeet Chief Lone Walker. She married early 19th-century mountain man Hugh Monroe, who joined the tribe, taking the name Rising Wolf. Reportedly he received the name for his habit of getting out of bed on his hands and knees. Rising Wolf Mountain is located two miles north of Sinopah on the opposite side of Two Medicine Lake, so the couple are still together in an appropriate location, with her mountain centered between those named for her husband and father. (Courtesy author.)

The author (left) is pictured along with Bill Wendt, Jerry Yenne, and Bill Orr, on the steep, winding trail to Triple Divide Pass in 1995. The sedimentary nature of most rock formations in Glacier National Park is clearly evident in this photograph. So too in the challenging task faced by those who built these trails, and those who maintain them. The author made his first trip across Triple Divide Pass with his father in 1962. In the background is the west face of 8,315-foot Medicine Grizzly Peak. (Courtesy Annalisa Yenne.)

OPPOSITE: This detail from a historic map of the lower East Side of Glacier National Park shows the relative locations of the Two Medicine and Cut Bank Valleys at a time when the Chalets were still operating at both locations. Also indicated are the roads leading into the valleys. On the right, the road north of Glacier Park Railroad Station (East Glacier) is now Montana Highway 49. U.S. Highway 2 runs along the park's southern edge and continues east from East Glacier. U.S. Highway 89 remains as shown here. In the upper left is Triple Divide Peak (now measured as 8,020 feet high), the only point in North America from which water drains into three oceans. At this point, the Continental Divide intersects the Hudson Bay Divide, which runs northeasterly from Triple Divide Peak through Divide Mountain (now measured as 8,665 feet) and on into Canada. Between the two divides north of Triple Divide, all the drainage is into the Arctic Ocean by way of the Saskatchewan River and Hudson Bay. See Appendix A for accurate elevations of higher mountains. This historic map is provided for general orientation, and to show the park as it appeared in the era when organized backcountry facilities, including the Chalets mentioned above and the Red Eagle Tent Camp, were at their peak. Today the backcountry facilities include more and simpler government-managed campgrounds designed for the use of backpackers and located throughout this region. (Detail from a 1940 U.S. Geological Survey map in the Yenne family collection.)

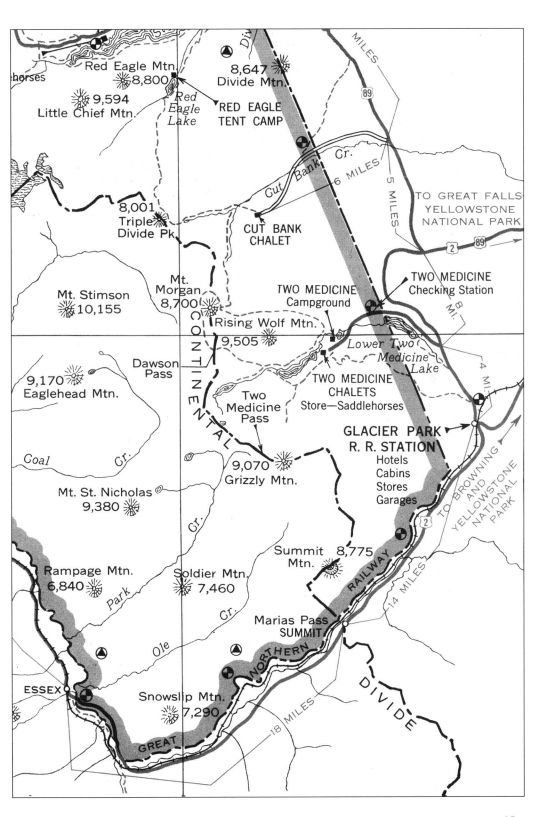

Atlantic Creek flows from the foot of Medicine Grizzly Lake, ultimately making its way to the Atlantic Ocean by way of Cut Bank Creek, and the Missouri and Mississippi Rivers. In the background is an excellent view of the glacial cirque formed against the north side of Medicine Grizzly Peak. (Photograph by Bill Yenne.)

The cold waters of Medicine Grizzly Lake shimmer in the sunlight. The head of the lake is at the foot of 8,610-foot Razoredge Mountain. According to Walter McClintock in his book *Old North Trail*, the legendary "Medicine Grizzly" was a large bear who once inhabited the upper Cut Bank Valley. McClintock explored the park as early as 1886 and was later adopted into the Blackfeet tribe, where he learned and recorded their legends and beliefs. (Photograph by Bill Yenne.)

The author's father, William J. Yenne, rides his favorite strawberry roan on the trail to Triple Divide Pass in this photograph taken August 11, 1962. Triple Divide Peak is in the background. (Courtesy Yenne family, from *Switchback* by William J. Yenne.)

OPPOSITE: Triple Divide Peak towers over 7,397-foot Triple Divide Pass. Dr. George Ruhle calls this 8,020-foot mountain "one of the most distinctive mountains in all North America." As he points out, no other point on the continent has drainage into three oceans, the Atlantic the Pacific and the Arctic. You can spill your canteen on its peak, and the water will drain into distant oceans thousands of miles apart. However, if you've climbed to the top, don't spill your water; you'll get thirsty on the way down. It lies between Continental Divide peaks Norris (8,882 feet) to the north and Razoredge to the south. To the east is Mount James (9,375 feet) and the continuation of the Hudson Bay Divide. To the right, Hudson Bay Creek drains eventually into the St. Mary River, then the Saskatchewan-Nelson river system, and into the Arctic Ocean by way of Hudson Bay. To the left, water flows into Medicine Grizzly Lake and the Mississippi-Missouri river system and ultimately into the Atlantic Ocean by way of the Gulf of Mexico. On the opposite side of the peak, Pacific Creek flows into the ocean of the same name by way of Nyack Creek, the Middle Fork of the Flathead River and the Columbia River system. (Courtesy Yenne family, from *Switchback* by William J. Yenne.)

Divide Mountain overlooks St. Mary from about five miles to the south. It stands 8,665 feet high and takes its name from its being on the crest of the Hudson Bay Divide. It is also on the boundary between the Blackfeet Reservation and Glacier National Park. (Photograph by Bill Yenne.)

Six

St. Mary

At the center of the East Side of Glacier National Park, there are the two St. Mary Lakes, less than a mile apart. Upper St. Many Lake, with its head deep within the bosom of the mountains, lies entirely within the park, while Lower St. Mary Lake lies on the Great Plains, entirely within the Blackfeet Reservation. Between them is the town of the same name.

The Blackfeet people called referred to the area as that of the "Walled-In Lakes," and the origin of the St. Mary name is uncertain. It is often credited to Fr. Pierre DeSmet, the Belgian Jesuit missionary who was active in what is now Western Montana and the Idaho panhandle in the 1840s, but there is no evidence that he ever saw the Walled-In Lakes. Other sources credit the naming to the 1870 Boundary Survey, or to Hugh Monroe (a.k.a. Rising Wolf), the 19th-century mountain man who married into the Blackfeet tribe.

Still the hub of the East Side, the town of St. Mary marks the point where the Going-to-the-Sun Road intersects U.S. Highway 89, and Upper St. Mary Lake provides the most recognized and most photographed view of Glacier (see pages 104–105). One of the places visited by George Bird Grinnell, the St. Mary Valley was also a natural location for Louis Hill to build a hotel. In fact, the Great Northern would build two in the area, one at the foot of Upper St. Mary Lake, and another near the head of the lake at Going-to-the-Sun Point (also known simply as Sun Point). Both would precede the development of the town of St. Mary, which evolved in the 1930s after the completion of the Going-to-the-Sun Road.

Located just inside the park and 36 miles from the Great Northern Railway Station at East Glacier, the St. Mary Chalets were of the same design as those at Two Medicine and Cut Bank, and were opened in 1913. The Going-to-the-Sun Chalets were a much larger and more ambitious project, centering on two large structures designed by Thomas McMahon and completed in 1915. The Going-to-the-Sun Chalets evolved from a tent camp known as Sun Camp that was first opened on the site in 1912. They were 10 miles deeper into the park than St. Mary Chalets, and reachable either by a saddle-horse trail, or from the foot of the lake aboard the 120-passenger vessel *St. Mary*.

As with Two Medicine and Many Glacier, the location of the Going-to-the-Sun Chalets offered spectacular views of the mountains, and served as a natural hub for the network of saddle-horse trails that spread across the East Side. During the 1920s, the Going-to-the-Sun Chalets and Sun Camp were the crossroads of the East Side, with hikers mingling with people who came by boat to bask in the majesty of the surroundings, or with people stopping off for a night as part of the ambitious Bar-X-6 saddle-horse tours across the part. In 1926, the already large complex was expanded further, with a new dining room and additional guest rooms.

The St. Mary Chalets, meanwhile, were less successful. As the Blackfeet Highway improved, it ceased to be a destination. People who arrived at East Glacier by train and who wanted to see the park would make either Many Glacier or the Going-to-the-Sun Chalets their destination.

Ironically, the death knell for the Going-to-the-Sun Chalets would be the highway of the same name. When the Going-to-the-Sun Road opened in 1933, people headed toward Logan Pass by

car now simply drove past the Chalets. The Great Northern met the need of those on car trips by constructing the East Glacier Cabin Camp, a motor inn complex began operation in 1941, four miles closer to St. Mary than the Going-to-the-Sun Chalets. It was located at Roes Creek and identified on some maps as the Roes Creek Campground. The creek was named for Charles Rose, with the alternate spelling being the result of a misprint on early maps.

All of the Glacier National Park visitor facilities were closed during World War II, and for both the St. Mary and Going-to-the-Sun Chalets, it would be for the last time. The former was torn down in 1943, the latter in 1948. The East Glacier Cabin Camp, however, reopened as the Rising Sun Motor Inn. It is still going strong to this day, having been enlarged from 19 to 72 units.

Just outside the park at the crossroads of the Going-to-the-Sun Road and Highway 89, the town of St. Mary thrived as a result of the new trans-park highway. In 1932, a former seasonal ranger from Michigan named Hugh Black and his wife Margaret started a small tourist development at the crossroads. They had a small store, six one-room cabins, and an eatery known as the Curly Bear Cafe. In 1952, the Blacks added to their complex with the opening of their 27-room St. Mary Lodge. Further additions and remodeling in 1975, 1989, and 1995 enlarged the hotel and added the Snowgoose Grill restaurant. Completed in 2001, the Great Bear Lodge added another 48 rooms to the complex now known as the Resort at Glacier. It is still owned and managed by the Black family.

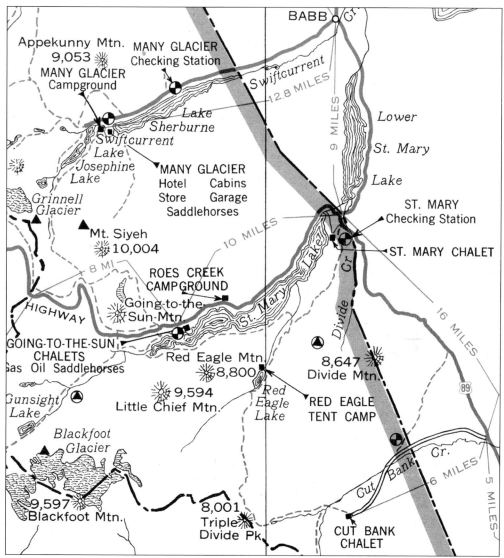

St. Mary is clearly the crossroads of the East Side of Glacier National Park. It is located at the intersection of the Going-to-the-Sun Road and U.S. Highway 89, formerly the Blackfeet Highway, which runs north-south just outside the eastern boundary of the park. This historic map of the central East Side of Glacier National Park centering on the two St. Mary Lakes is provided for general orientation, and to show the park as it appeared in the era when organized backcountry facilities were at their peak. Red Eagle Tent Camp, as well as the St. Mary, Cut Bank and Going-to-the-Sun Chalets did not survive the 1940s, but the Roes Creek Campground is still in operation as the Rising Sun Motor Inn. The National Park Service also operates vehicle accessible campgrounds at Rising Sun and St. Mary, and there are backcountry campgrounds available for hikers at Red Eagle Lake and throughout the region. See Appendix A for accurate elevations of higher mountains. (Detail from a 1940 U.S. Geological Survey map in the Yenne family collection.)

Opposite: This view looks south across Upper St. Mary Lake toward 8,099-foot Curly Bear Mountain—just east of 8,881-foot-tall Red Eagle Mountain. (Photograph by Bill Yenne.)

Pictured is the St. Mary Lodge as it appeared early one morning in August 1979, before the recent additions. Divide Mountain can be seen in the distance. (Photograph by Bill Yenne.)

This photograph from the 1920s shows a pair of the Great Northern Railway's White touring cars on the Blackfeet Highway as they descend the West Side of the Hudson Bay Divide. The distinctive peaks at Upper St. Mary Lake are visible in the distance. (Courtesy author.)

OPPOSITE: Singleshot Mountain is the first peak that one passes when driving into the park on the Going-to-the-Sun Road from the East Entrance. The 7,926-foot peak was so named by James Willard Schultz when George Bird Grinnell shot a bighorn ram here with a single shot. (Photograph by Bill Yenne.)

ABOVE: Decked out in their riding gear, tourists head toward St. Mary after a happy stay at the Going-to-the-Sun Chalets. Before the Going-to-the-Sun Road, the only way to get to Sun Point and the Chalets was by boat. (Courtesy author.)

OPPOSITE ABOVE: Upper St. Mary Lake is unusually calm in this view of Going-to-the-Sun Chalets from the 1920s. The Chalets were completed in 1915, but there still appears to be some construction work ongoing. The nearest peaks are 8,084-foot Dusty Star Mountain on the left, and 9,642-foot Going-to-the-Sun Mountain on the right. (Courtesy author.)

OPPOSITE BELOW: This photograph of Going-to-the-Sun Chalets shows the property at its heyday in the 1930s, when it was still the hub of the East Side's Inside Trail system that stretched 45 miles from here to Two Medicine Lake. With the opening of the Going-to-the-Sun Road in 1933, however, more and more park visitors brought their own vehicles, and bypassed the Chalets. They were closed during World War II and they never reopened. (Courtesy author.)

97

Virginia Falls is located on the creek of the same name, one of several major streams that flow off the Continental Divide into the head of Upper St. Mary Lake. It is nearly 14 trail miles from St. Mary, but less than two from the Going-to-the-Sun Road. (Photograph by Bill Yenne.)

The dominant theme adopted by Louis Hill for his Glacier National Park hostelries was that of the Swiss chalet. The architecture was inspired by the Swiss, and, in the 1930s, so too were the uniforms worn by the service staff. These young ladies were photographed by National Park Service photographer George Alexander Grant at the Going-to-the-Sun Chalets on Upper St. Mary Lake on July 5, 1933. The cloud-topped peak directly behind them is 8,084-foot Dusty Star Mountain, one of St. Mary's most recognizable landmarks. (Courtesy National Park Service.)

Red Eagle Lake is located at an elevation of 4,722 feet in the valley that parallels that of Upper St. Mary Lake. The lake, as well as the creek running from it and the nearby mountain and glacier, are all named for Red Eagle, the uncle of James Willard Schultz's Blackfeet wife. Schultz generously named these features for Red Eagle when the man saved the life of the Schultzes' son. (Courtesy National Park Service.)

Note the Bar-X-6 brand on both of the horses in this 1920s Joe Scheuerle illustration. During the 1920s and 1930s, the Bar-X-6 saddle-horse company had over 1,000 head of horses and more than 100 employees. During the 1930s, it was not uncommon to see saddle-horse parties of nearly 100 riders. The Bar-X-6 was formed in 1917 by W. N. Noffsinger, who bought out an earlier saddle-horse operator, the Brewster Transportation Company, based at Canada's Banff National Park. The story of the Bar-X-6 and other early saddle-horse operations is told in more detail in the book *Switchback* by W. J. Yenne. (Courtesy author.)

Red Eagle Mountain, with an elevation of 8,881 feet, is on the north side of the lake of the same name, lying between it and Upper St. Mary Lake. (Courtesy National Park Service.)

Opened in 1926 at the foot of the lake, Red Eagle Camp was a popular stopover during the golden age of the large Bar-X-6 horse parties on the Inside Trail. After World War II, that activity had faded from popularity, and the camp was never reopened. It was about eight trail miles from St. Mary, and 15 trail miles from Cut Bank by way of Triple Divide Pass. The Bar-X-6 operated several such camps, including those at Fifty Mountain and Crossley (now Cosley) Lake on the popular North Circle Trail north of Many Glacier. (Courtesy author.)

Traveling westward on the Going-to-the-Sun Road along the north side of upper St. Mary Lake, one can look nearly straight up at such lofty peaks such as 8,826-foot Goat Mountain and 9,642-foot Going-to-the-Sun Mountain. (Photograph by Bill Yenne.)

Little Chief Mountain is one of the many spectacular peaks visible on the south side of Upper St. Mary Lake as one travels westward toward Logan Pass on the Going-to-the-Sun Road. With an elevation of 9,541 feet, Little Chief is actually 459 feet taller than legendary Chief Mountain. It was named by George Bird Grinnell in 1887 to commemorate Maj. Frank North, leader of the U.S. Army's Pawnee Scout detachment. North's Pawnee nickname translated as Little Chief. (Photograph by Bill Yenne.)

This amusing cartoon depicts tourists and wranglers departing the Going-to-the-Sun Chalets aboard the motor launch *St. Mary*. (Courtesy author.)

Little Chief Mountain looms high over Upper St. Mary Lake. The buildings on the point across the lake were torn down before the 1960s. (Courtesy author.)

Perhaps the most recognized image of Glacier National Park is the view of Upper St. Mary Lake from the narrows, about 44 miles on the Going-to-the-Sun Road from the West Entrance and seven from the East Entrance at St. Mary. A favorite of both amateur and professional photographers, this view is dominated by tiny Wild Goose Island, so named because it was once a stopping place for Canada geese. The island was also once used by the Blackfeet people for ceremonial purposes. The mountains include Mahtotopa, Little Chief, and Dusty Star on the left, and the shoulder of Going-to-the-Sun Mountain on the right. The tall, pointed peak in the center is 8,750-foot Fusillade Mountain near Logan Pass. George Bird Grinnell named it in 1891 when W. H. Seward and future secretary of state Henry L. Stimson failed to hit anything when they fired a fusillade of rifle rounds at a group of mountain goats on the slopes of the peak. (Photograph by Bill Yenne.)

Pictured is the Prince of Wales Hotel with 7,802-foot Mount Crandall as a backdrop. When it opened in 1927, the hotel brought a tourism boom to Waterton, which had been greatly overshadowed by the parks farther north in Alberta, such as Banff and Lake Louise. (Courtesy author.)

Here is Chief Mountain Customs, the Canadian Port of Entry southeast of Waterton as it appeared soon after the completion of the Chief Mountain International Highway in 1935. Long-since paved, the 39-mile road connects Waterton with U.S. Highway 89 at Babb, Montana. The border monument down the road in the background with the twin flagpoles still stands. (Courtesy author.)

Seven

WATERTON LAKES NATIONAL PARK

Across the Alberta border, and contiguous with Glacier National Park, is Waterton Lakes National Park, named for British naturalist Charles Waterton. It was Canada's fourth national park. Now comprising 129,920 acres, it evolved from a 34,559-acre section of land set aside in 1895 by the Canadian government at the suggestion of Pincher Creek rancher F. W. Godsal. The centerpiece of the park are the three Waterton Lakes. The Middle and Lower Waterton Lakes are entirely within the province of Alberta, while Upper Waterton Lake (usually called simply Waterton Lake) straddles the international boundary. The tour boat that operates on this lake is known as the *International*.

Like Glacier National Park, Waterton Lakes comprises several disparate ecological zones, and many different habitat types, including grasslands, shrublands, wetlands, lakes, spruce-fir, pine and aspen forests, and alpine areas. This makes both parks unusually rich and varied for their size.

As noted earlier in this book, the governments of the two nations chose in 1932 to officially refer to the two neighboring parks as the Waterton-Glacier International Peace Park, and they were together designated as a World Heritage Site in 1995, because they represent an "outstanding example representing significant ongoing ecological and biological processes."

The Waterton town site, situated at the foot of Upper Waterton Lake, has a seasonal population of 2,000, making it the largest town contained within the boundary of either park.

In 1913, the Great Northern Railway's Louis Hill proposed building another hotel—in the spirit of Glacier Park and Many Glacier—on the bluff overlooking the Waterton town site. Delayed by World War I, this project finally got underway in 1926, and Hill's third grand hotel opened in July 1927 overlooking Waterton town site. It was named for Edward, Prince of Wales (later King Edward VIII), the popular heir apparent to the British throne who owned property near Waterton.

This roadside boundary marker is located adjacent to the border crossing that is pictured on the opposite page. The swath of cut trees in the background marks the boundary between the two countries. (Photograph by Bill Yenne.)

ABOVE: This is an early aerial view of Upper Waterton Lake, looking south toward the mountains of Glacier National Park. The Prince of Wales Hotel, perched on its imposing bluff, overlooks the Waterton town site. In the center in the distance is 10,466-foot Mount Cleveland, Glacier's tallest peak. On the right are Cathedral Peaks and Mount Campbell. (Courtesy author.)

OPPOSITE ABOVE: The southern end of Waterton Lake in Glacier National Park is pictured in the 1930s. The Goat Haunt Chalet was built near here in 1924 by Waterton entrepreneurs Henry Hanson and Walter Morrow, and sold to the Bar-X-6 saddle-horse company a year later. It served as a stopping place on the North Circle Trail until 1941, when it was closed. (Courtesy author.)

OPPOSITE BELOW: This 1920s photograph looks east from the Akamina Highway, across Waterton town site, toward 7,825-foot Vimy Peak. Originally Observation Peak, the peak was renamed for the Battle of Vimy Ridge in World War I, during which Canadian forces achieved a victory over the Germans. Beginning on Easter Monday in April 1917, the battle is important in Canadian history for being the first time that the nation's army fought a major battle as an integral unit. The 30,000 soldiers who fought there were from throughout Canada, so their victory furthered Canadian national unity. (Courtesy author.)

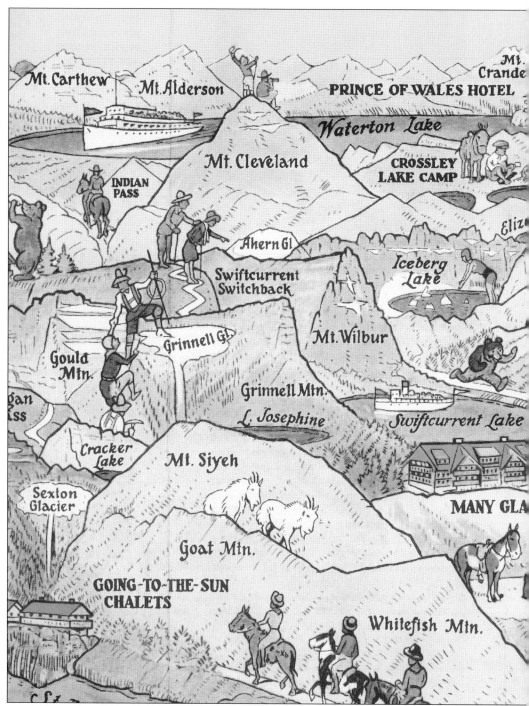

This Joseph Scheuerle illustration from the *Vacations for All* brochure contains an amazing panorama of the entire upper East Side of Glacier, with Waterton and the Prince of Wales Hotel top center. In the middle is the Many Glacier Hotel and Swiftcurrent Lake, with a touring car full of eager guests arriving. In the upper left, the motor vessel *International* takes passengers for a cruise on Waterton Lake while climbers atop Mount Cleveland wave to them. Other mountaineers

are ascending Grinnell Glacier. The Chief Mountain Customs and their namesake peak are in the upper right. Going-to-the-Sun Chalets and St. Mary Lake are in the lower left. Hikers and saddle-horse groups are scattered throughout the landscape. Although this fanciful illustration dates to the 1920s, the sights and many of the activities pictured here are still awaiting visitors today. (Courtesy author.)

The 7,700-foot peak of Grinnell Point rises majestically above Swiftcurrent Lake opposite the Many Glacier Hotel. (Photograph by Bill Yenne.)

Eight

MANY GLACIER

Nine miles north of St. Mary and about 26 miles south of Waterton town site, Swiftcurrent Creek flows into the foot of Lower St. Mary Lake. Following Swiftcurrent Creek westward and back into Glacier National Park, one reaches Swiftcurrent Lake, a dozen miles upstream from Lower St. Mary Lake. Here is one of the most remarkable natural amphitheaters ever carved by ancient glacial action.

Opposite Swiftcurrent Lake, Grinnell Point looms large, and on either side of it, alpine valleys recede into the distance, each containing a chain of lakes. On the right, Swiftcurrent Creek flows down through Fishercap, Redrock, and Bullhead Lakes, having originated from Swiftcurrent Glacier. A fork to the right off Swiftcurrent Creek is Wilbur Creek, which can be followed to Iceberg Lake. North of Iceberg Lake is the dramatic Ptarmigan Wall. The 183-foot Ptarmigan Tunnel, bored through this steep wall of rock in 1930, still ranks as one of the greatest backcountry engineering projects in the national park system. W. J. Yenne describes the tunnel project in detail in his book *Switchback*.

South of Swiftcurrent Lake, one may hike to Lake Josephine and beyond to Grinnell Lake, with Grinnell Glacier above. It was at Swiftcurrent Lake, originally known as Lake McDermott, that George Bird Grinnell first beheld the majesty of Glacier, and it was from here that he hiked to the lake and glacier that bear his name. It was also at Swiftcurrent Lake, a generation later, that the Great Northern Railway's Louis Hill decided to build his largest and grandest lodge.

Hill had selected the site, which he described as being like Switzerland, in 1909. During the summer of 1913, he had eight small Swiss-style chalets in service at Many Glacier, and the following year work began on the great lodge. The architect was Thomas McMahon, but Louis Hill himself was intimately involved in the design process. Unlike the Glacier Park Lodge, which used timber from the Pacific Northwest, the Many Glacier Hotel was built almost entirely with cedar and other materials from the local area. Most of the hotel's woodwork, including furniture, utilized native timber. The stone foundation for Many Glacier was also built with local rock. More than 2 million board feet of lumber was cut from the forest east of the hotel, with a sawmill built on the site to turn out finished lumber. In fact, the only fully pre-finished woodwork brought to the hotel site were window sashes and door frames.

The Many Glacier Hotel opened on July 4, 1915. It may have had a rustic appearance, but it was outfitted with comforts and conveniences such as telephones, hot and cold running water, steam heat, and electric lights. As with the Glacier Park Lodge, the basic facility was augmented by additional buildings, which were completed in 1918. Not only is the 208-room Many Glacier Hotel the largest hostelry in or near Glacier National Park, it was, for many years, the largest hotel anywhere in Montana. Today the Swiss theme is still very prominent throughout the hotel, especially in the main dining room, which features the flags of Switzerland's Cantons, and in the Interlaken Lounge.

As had been the case at other Great Northern sites on the East Side of Glacier National Park, the completion of the hotel had been preceded by the establishment of a tent camp in 1911, using tents modeled after Blackfeet tipis. This camp was located at the opposite side of Swiftcurrent Lake, near where Upper Swiftcurrent Creek flows into it, and a campground remains in the area to this day. In 1933, the Great Northern constructed 27 cabins near this location, and these became known as the Many Glacier Auto Tourist Camp. A camp store and other facilities were between 1935 and 1940, and in 1955, motel units were added to what is now known as the Swiftcurrent Motor Inn.

ABOVE: Mount Wilbur is pictured with a meadow of wildflowers in the foreground. (Courtesy author.)

Many Glacier Region, Glacier Park

The Old West for a new vacation—Glacier Park!

The glamour of frontier days still clings to this land of shining mountains—rough-and-ready sports, adventure, old-time hospitality. Ride up a mile and back a hundred years—yet find yourself each night in a comfortable mountain hotel or chalet. Come out where vacations seem different—and you do too! Summer fares from the East are lowest ever. Write Great Northern Vacations, Dept. J-5, St. Paul, Minn.

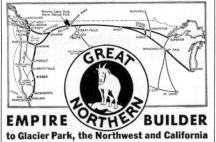

EMPIRE GREAT NORTHERN **BUILDER**
to Glacier Park, the Northwest and California

LEFT: This Great Northern Railway advertisement promoted the notion of a vacation in Glacier National Park, and offered the deluxe *Empire Builder* passenger train as the ideal way to get there. In 1932, when this ad appeared, reliable paved roads from east to west were still in the future, so the train was pretty much the *only* way to reach Glacier from either Seattle or St. Paul. The illustration shows a couple of young tourists looking down upon the Many Glacier Hotel from the slopes of Altyn Peak. The trail was built in 1922. (Courtesy author.)

OPPOSITE ABOVE: This photograph from the side of 7,947-foot Mount Altyn provides an excellent overview of the Swiftcurrent Lake area, with the Many Glacier Hotel on the left and Grinnell Point on the right. The mountain on the left is 9,376-foot Allen Mountain, and in the center is 9,553-foot Mount Gould, with the Garden Wall forming its shoulders. The Going-to-the-Sun Road is on the opposite side. (Courtesy author.)

OPPOSITE BELOW: A Bar-X-6 saddle-horse party prepares to head out from the Many Glacier Hotel in the 1920s. Today outfitters still offer saddle-horse trips from Many Glacier to locations in the surrounding valleys, including the trip to Josephine Lake, with its remarkable view of Grinnell Glacier. (Courtesy author.)

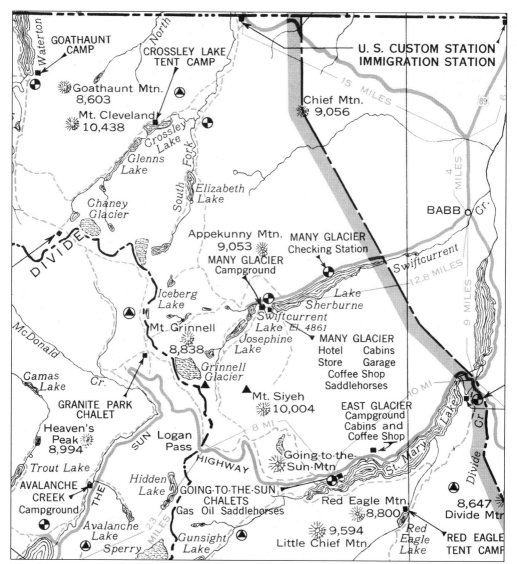

This historic map centering on Swiftcurrent Lake and the Many Glacier area shows it as the nexus for many glacial valleys, filled with chains of stunning alpine lakes, such as Josephine and Iceberg, with glaciers such as Grinnell their heads. At the top of the map are the Canadian border and the southern end of Waterton Lake. The backcountry camps at Goat Haunt and at Crossley (now Cosley) Lake were important stops on the North Circle saddle-horse tour. Today there are backcountry campgrounds available for hikers at these two locations and elsewhere throughout the region. Swiftcurrent Creek drains from the lake of the same name into—and out of—Lake Sherburne. The latter lies almost entirely within the park, but it is formed by a dam located outside of the park. The dam was approved before the park was created. Mount Cleveland, the highest point in the park, is now confirmed to have an elevation of 10,466 feet. See Appendix A for accurate elevations of higher mountains. This historic map is provided for general orientation, and to show the park as it appeared in the era when organized backcountry facilities were at their peak. Today the backcountry facilities include more and simpler government-managed campgrounds designed for the use of backpackers. (Detail from a 1940 U.S. Geological Survey map in the Yenne family collection.)

Iceberg Creek leads to Iceberg Lake, which is located at an elevation of 6,094 feet. Filling an entire glacial cirque, it is surrounded on three sides by 3,000-foot vertical cliffs. Because of this, it remains in shade and frozen nearly all year. Icebergs remain even in the warmest weeks of summer. (Courtesy author.)

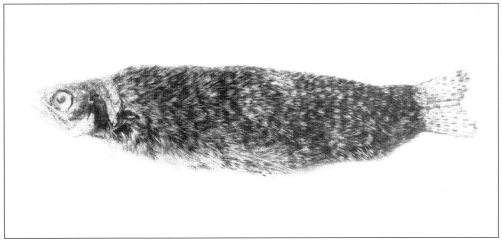

One of Glacier's most enduring legends is that of Iceberg Lake being so cold that the trout grew fur. First described to gullible tourists by tall-tale-telling saddle-horse guides in the 1920s, the yarn took on a life of its own. In about 1932, the myth was embraced by the legendary photographer Roy E. "Ted" Marble, who commissioned a taxidermist to outfit a trout with a ground squirrel pelt. Marble's practical joke became a best-selling postcard. The producer of thousands of serious photographic postcards, Marble operated a studio near the west entrance of the park for two decades, until his death in 1938. Mrs. Marble was the author's second-grade teacher at West Glacier School. (Courtesy author.)

ABOVE: Run-off from Grinnell Glacier, high on the Garden Wall above, spills into Grinnell Lake then runs eastward into Lake Josephine and eventually into the Arctic Ocean. The opacity of such lakes is derived from "glacial milk," or *gletschermilch*, a fine dust created by glacial action and suspended in the water. (Photograph by Bill Yenne.)

OPPOSITE ABOVE: Glacier's tallest peak, 10,466-foot Mount Cleveland, rises over Cosley Lake, located in the Belly River country north of Many Glacier. Named for Joe Cosley, an early mountain man and ranger, the lake was identified on maps for many years as "Crossley" Lake. (Courtesy author.)

OPPOSITE BELOW: The author took this photograph of Grinnell Glacier in July 1998. The upper lobe of the glacier on the ledge above is known as the Salamander. (Courtesy author.)

This wary bighorn sheep (*Ovis canadensis*) was photographed by the author on the shelf adjacent to Grinnell Glacier. The sheep are common throughout the high country of Glacier National Park, but usually do not venture as close to the roads as do the mountain goats. (Photograph by Bill Yenne.)

Looking southwest toward Cosley Lake from the Crossley Ridge Lookout. (Courtesy National Park Service via U.S. Geological Survey.)

Bullhead Lake lies at the head of the Swiftcurrent Valley and at the base of the eastern side of the Garden Wall. The pleasant, level walk from here to Swiftcurrent Lake is in contrast to the steep climb from here, across the Continental Divide, to Granite Park Chalets. (Photograph by Bill Yenne.)

Pictured are stalks of bear grass (*Xerophyllum tenax*), the delicate flowering plant that is widely seen throughout the meadows of Glacier's high country each summer. It is neither a grass, nor is it eaten by bears. Glacier's signature flower is actually a perennial in the lily family, with stalks that often grow to four feet or taller. (Photograph by Bill Yenne.)

...Can Heaven More Beautiful Be?

Tributes to Glacier have been many, but one of the author's favorites is the "Glacier Park Song," with words and music composed by Clarence Emory Cunningham in 1955. I still recall my mother playing it on the piano in our home in Park Headquarters many long years ago. The refrain says it all—"Can Heaven more beautiful be?"

GLACIER PARK SONG

Words and Music by
CLARENCE EMORY CUNNINGHAM

There's a gar - den in the sky, where the sun and stars go by, A ma jes - tic land of peace and har - mon - y._____ And ech - oes from her laugh - ing rills, temp - le spires and wood - ed hills, come to bring me A sweet mel - o - dy._____

In the Rock - y Moun - tains, be - low the gar - den wall, there's a land, the

124

fair-est to see, _____ Where the sun shines bright-ly on gla-cier wat-er-

fall, roll-ing down to the great crys-tal sea. _____ I stand, I

gaze, I won-der; _____ Can Heav-en more beau-ti-ful be? _____

In this land of glor-y, I love to ling-er on, And join in the

Glac - ier Park Song. _____ In the Song.

Appendix A: Prominent Peaks Denoted on U.S. Geological Survey Quadrangle Maps for Glacier National Park

(Source: U.S. Geological Survey, thanks to Carl Key and Richard Menicke. Data from other sources may vary.)

Mountain	Elevation in feet		
Mount Cleveland	10,466	Chief Mountain	9,080
Mount Stimson	10,142	Mount Edwards	9,072
Kintla Peak	10,110	Appekuny (Apikuni) Mountain	9,068
Mount Jackson	10,052	Grizzly Mountain	9,067
Mount Siyeh	10,014	Cathedral Peak	9,041
Mount Merritt	10,004	Citadel Mountain	9,030
Long Knife Peak	9,910	Parke Peak	9,010
Rainbow Peak	9,890	Heavens Peak	8,987
Mount Carter	9,843	Mount Cannon	8,952
Kinnerly Peak	9,810	Walton Mountain	8,926
Going-to-the-Sun Mountain	9,642	Almost-A-Dog Mountain	8,922
Vulture Peak	9,638	Seward Mountain	8,917
Ipasha Peak	9,572	Crowfeet Mountain	8,914
Blackfoot Mountain	9,574	Longfellow Peak	8,904
Mount Gould	9,553	Whitecalf Mountain	8,893
Little Chief Mountain	9,541	Mount Custer	8,883
Rising Wolf Mountain	9,513	Norris Mountain	8,882
Mount Phillips	9,494	Red Eagle Mountain	8,881
Kaina Mountain	9,489	Miche Wabun Peak	8,861
Natoas Peak	9,476	Mount Grinnell*	8,851
Chapman Peak	9,406	Mount Vaught	8,850
Red Mountain	9,377	Mount Henry	8,847
Mount Saint Nicholas	9,376	Bear Mountain	8,841
Mount Allen	9,376	South Iceberg Peak	8,840
Mount James	9,375	Mount Kipp	8,839
The Guardhouse	9,336	The Sentinel**	8,835
Mount Wilbur	9,321	Mount Alderson	8,832
Mount Pinchot	9,310	Battlement Mountain	8,830
Mount Rockwell	9,272	Goat Mountain	8,826
Gable Mountain	9,262	Church Butte	8,808
Gunsight Mountain	9,258	Yellow Mountain	8,766
Mount Logan	9,239	Numa Peak	8,710
Flinsch Peak	9,225		
Piegan Mountain	9,220		
Mount Peabody	9,210		
Pollock Mountain	9,190	* Not to be confused with 7,600-foot	
Iceberg Peak	9,145	Grinnell Point	
Eaglehead Mountain	9,140		
Bishops Cap	9,127	** Not to be confused with 8,245-foot	
Reynolds Mountain	9,125	Mount Sentinel	
Stoney Indian Peaks	9,110		

APPENDIX B: THE LARGEST GLACIERS IN GLACIER NATIONAL PARK

The first column lists estimated glacier sizes at the end of the "Little Ice Age," c. 1850. The second column refers to the primary glacial patch at the time of source year (in parentheses). The last column lists the total number of glacial patches now associated with that glacier. The areas are in square kilometers. (Source: U.S. Geological Survey.)

Blackfoot	7.59*	1.74 (1979)	3
Rainbow	n/a	1.21 (1966)	6
Harrison	3.09	1.06 (1993)	18
Agassiz	4.06	1.02 (1993)	10
Jackson	(3.44)*	1.02 (1979)	23
Grinnell	2.33**	.88 (1993)	6
Sperry	3.76	.87 (1993)	7
Pumpelly	1.84	.72 (1979)	9
Kintla	n/a	.66 (1966)	13
Ahern	n/a	.59 (1966)	10

* The area for Blackfoot Glacier encompasses what is now Jackson Glacier. The area reported for Jackson Glacier in column one is the estimated portion of Blackfoot Glacier that later formed Jackson Glacier after the two became separate glaciers. (Source: U.S. Geological Survey.)
** The area for Grinnell Glacier in column one encompasses a now-separate ice apron now known as the Salamander.

APPENDIX C: SELECTED MAJOR FOREST FIRES IN GLACIER NATIONAL PARK

YEAR	NAME	ACRES BURNED*
1910	Anaconda Creek	27,000 **
1929	Halfmoon	39,809
1936	Heavens Peak	7,500
1958	Coal Creek	2,534
1988	Red Bench	27,500
1998	Kootenai	8,758
1999	Anaconda	10,812
2001	Moose	27,194
2003	Robert	39,400
2003	Wedge Canyon	30,300
2003	Rampage	21,000
2003	Trapper Creek	18,700

* Acreage within the park. Many fires, especially those in 1910, 1929, and 2003, also burned substantial acreage outside the park boundaries.
** The Anaconda Creek fire was just one of several fires that burned a total of 65,000 acres within the park in 1910.
The source for the 10 largest fires was Dennis Divoky of the Glacier National Park Fire Management Office. The source for the others is *Through the Years in Glacier National Park: An Administrative History* by Donald Robinson (1960).

APPENDIX D: GLACIER'S TALLEST WATERFALLS

NAME	HEIGHT	LOCATION
Avalanche Basin Falls	2,320 feet	Avalanche Lake
Monument Falls	1,840 feet	Avalanche Lake
Frances Lake Falls	1,680 feet	Lake Frances
Beaver Chief Falls	1,291 feet	Lake Ellen Wilson
Bird Woman Falls	960 feet	Logan Pass
Floral Park Falls	960 feet	Avalanche Lake
Grinnel Falls	960 feet	Grinnell Lake
Hole-in-the-Wall Falls	800 feet	Livingstone Ridge

"Can Heaven more beautiful be?" Snow-covered Heaven's Peak appears to be one with this boiling cumulus cloud on a cold morning, as summer comes to Glacier's high country. (Photograph by Bill Yenne.)

Your experience in this blessed land may well become the richest in the treasure-house of memory as you move from the giddy everyday world into the pristine purity of nature. Here you are drawn very close to the Creator as you gaze into the blue depth of unpolluted skies, feel the might of a mountain as you stand on its summit, or let your eyes drift over an endless expanse of plains breaking against the base of the ranges. No soporific drug is needed to lull you as winds sough in the treetops, as waves lap in unbroken succession on a pebbled shore, as a merry stream sings between shining boulders in its path.

—Dr. George C. Ruhle